IMAGES
of America

POINT PIEDRAS BLANCAS

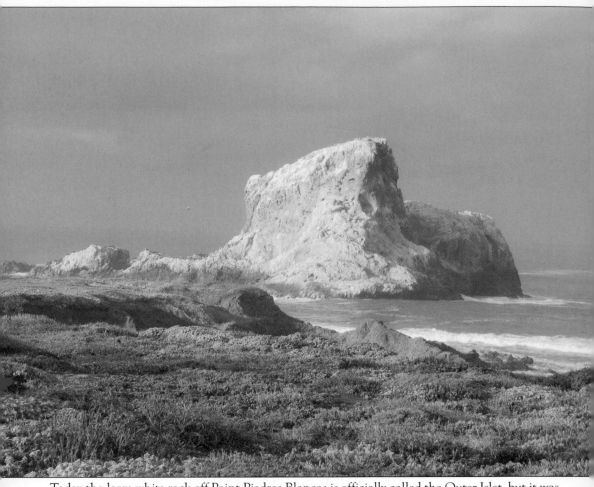

Today the large white rock off Point Piedras Blancas is officially called the Outer Islet, but it was formerly known as Piedra Blanca, or "white rock." Piedra Blanca lent its name to the rancho that once included this portion of the coast. Along with other large white rocks in the vicinity, it is the inspiration for the name of the area, Point Piedras Blancas. (Photograph by Carole Adams.)

IMAGES
of America

POINT PIEDRAS BLANCAS

Carole Adams and John Bogacki

ARCADIA
PUBLISHING

Copyright © 2008 by Carole Adams and John Bogacki
ISBN 978-0-7385-5819-6

Published by Arcadia Publishing
Charleston SC, Chicago IL, Portsmouth NH, San Francisco CA

Printed in the United States of America

Library of Congress Catalog Card Number: 2007941837

For all general information contact Arcadia Publishing at:
Telephone 843-853-2070
Fax 843-853-0044
E-mail sales@arcadiapublishing.com
For customer service and orders:
Toll-Free 1-888-313-2665

Visit us on the Internet at www.arcadiapublishing.com

We would like to dedicate this book to all the keepers who tended the Piedras Blancas light and to the volunteers, friends, and visionaries working together to keep the lantern shining.

CONTENTS

ACKNOWLEDGMENTS

The photographs and images used in this book came from a variety of sources. Many were generously donated to the Piedras Blancas Light Station, which is managed by the Bureau of Land Management (BLM). Most of the photographs have come from individuals, organizations, or agencies, including the U.S. Lighthouse Society, the U.S. Coast Guard, the Nautical Research Centre, National Marine Fisheries Service, and the Maritime Museum of Monterey. Individuals who have contributed photographs include Donna Jean Schneider, Pat Inabnit, Jan Mattson, Jim Godsey, Shirley Null, Elinor DeWire, Robert Schwemmer, Donald Seelhorst, Marjorie Sewell, Florence Gonzales, Neil Hansen, Susan Wright, Morgan Lynn, Brian Hatfield, Suzanne Dallons, Michael L. Baird, John Bogacki, Carole and Phil Adams, and more than we can list in this space. We would like to thank everyone who so generously shared in providing us with a glimpse into the fascinating past of Point Piedras Blancas. We hope our collection of photographs and information will grow. If you have an image or information you would like to share, contact Piedras Blancas Light Station, P.O. Box 129, San Simeon, CA 93452-129 or phone 805-927-2968.

Proceeds from the sale of this book go to the Piedras Blancas Light Station Association (PBLSA), the nonprofit organization responsible for raising funds to support the restoration of the Piedras Blancas Light Station. For more information, contact Piedras Blancas Light Station Association, P.O. Box 127, San Simeon, CA 93452-127 or phone 805-927-3719.

The authors wish to express their appreciation to everyone who contributed information or images and to the Bureau of Land Management and the Piedras Blancas Light Station Association. Special thanks go to John McGarry, Jerry Praver, Mary Bogacki, and Phil Adams for their assistance and support.

Visit the BLM Web site, www.piedrasblancas.gov, or the PBLSA Web site at www.piedrasblancas. org for more information.

INTRODUCTION

Piedras Blancas is a rugged, windswept point located along California's central coast, near San Simeon. Blended together in a dramatic meeting of land and sea is a saga comprised of human and natural history.

The human history of Point Piedras Blancas began long ago. An archaeological examination of the site conducted in October 2005 yielded an artifact about 3,300 years old, although the site was probably used by Native Americans prior to that. After the arrival of the Europeans, Point Piedras Blancas was part of Mission San Miguel and later became part of Rancho Piedra Blanca. Piedras Blancas means "white rocks" in Spanish.

Following the Gold Rush, there was a dramatic increase in coastal shipping, and it was necessary to construct lighthouses as aids to navigation. Two shipwrecks occurred just north of Point Piedras Blancas in 1869, highlighting the need for a lighthouse at Point Piedras Blancas. In April 1874, the U.S. Lighthouse Establishment began construction of the lighthouse, and in less than 10 months, the structure was completed. The first-order Fresnel lens was lit for the first time on February 15, 1875. A two-story Victorian house was built in 1876 to house the keepers and their families. In 1906, a fog signal building and a head keeper's dwelling were added.

In 1939, the U.S. Coast Guard absorbed the U.S. Lighthouse Service, including responsibility for coastal navigation and maritime safety. During that period, many changes were made at light stations, including Piedras Blancas. Earthquake damage over the years made it necessary to remove the upper portion of the tower in 1949, including the lantern room and the first-order Fresnel lens. The Victorian-era keeper's quarters were removed in 1960 and replaced with a row of four ranch-style block houses, sturdy enough to withstand the blustery winds associated with Piedras Blancas. In 1975, the station became automated, and it was no longer necessary to house personnel on site.

In 1977, after the station became unmanned, biologists from the U.S. Fish and Wildlife Service applied for and received permission from the coast guard to occupy the site and establish a biological research center. For almost 25 years, Point Piedras Blancas served as an active research center.

Piedras Blancas continues to host a broad spectrum of research projects, including the biannual range-wide southern sea otter census, the collection of sea otter stranding data for the entire state, and information on the local Piedras Blancas elephant seal rookery by the U.S. Geological Survey. The site also hosts the annual gray whale cow/calf survey by National Marine Fisheries Service. Other ongoing research includes tide pool monitoring by the Partnership for Interdisciplinary Studies of Coastal Oceans (PISCO) and National Oceanic and Atmospheric Administration (NOAA) weather gathering.

In October 2001, the Bureau of Land Management assumed management of the Piedras Blancas Light Station (PBLS). This change in management and stewardship signaled an exciting, positive change in the destiny of this amazing site.

One of the reasons the BLM assumed management of the Piedras Blancas Light Station was the creation of the California Coastal National Monument in 2000. The monument, which is comprised of rocks and islands off the California coastline, is also managed by the BLM. Piedras Blancas was chosen as an interpretive "gateway" to educate the public about the monument's attributes. BLM offers public tours on a limited basis, which will undoubtedly increase. Even in its decapitated condition, the lighthouse beckons the public, who pass by on busy, scenic Highway 1.

Before the upper portion of the tower was removed, it was undoubtedly one of the most architecturally significant lighthouses along the entire West Coast. Today the lighthouse and the entire light station stand in need of repair. The BLM has completed a comprehensive site management plan, which identifies a significant site restoration program that will include restoration of the lighthouse and historic buildings, as well as natural area restoration. To assist with this project, a nonprofit organization, the Piedras Blancas Light Station Association, has been formed and is charged with raising the funds necessary to support BLM's restoration efforts. The light station will be restored to its period of historic significance, which was 1874–1940.

A major vegetative miracle is occurring at the Piedras Blancas Light Station thanks to the hard work of dedicated BLM volunteers, supported by staff and the community. Invasive ice plant, native to South Africa, was introduced to the site around 1940 and in following years. It had formed an almost continuous carpet by the time the BLM assumed management. In just five years, the majority of the 19-acre site has been cleared of ice plant and native plants are flourishing. The result is a return of a more natural ecosystem.

The recent exploding growth of the elephant seal population at Piedras Blancas has received national and worldwide attention. The Piedras Blancas rookery has become the largest mainland elephant seal rookery. Tens of thousands of visitors are drawn to the Point Piedras Blancas area to view these wild creatures every year. In addition, there is an abundance of other marine life to be viewed at Piedras Blancas, including sea otters, harbor seals, California sea lions, and a variety of cetaceans. One of the birds to regularly nest on the large rock just offshore is the peregrine falcon. It can frequently be seen sitting on the tower.

This book offers the reader a glimpse into the human and natural history that come together at Point Piedras Blancas. It is a look into the past, but hopefully it will also provide a hint of what the future may hold for this special place.

One

BEFORE THE LIGHT

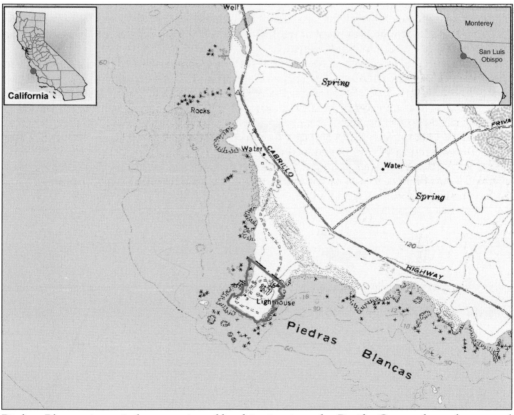

Piedras Blancas is a windswept point of land jutting into the Pacific Ocean along the central coast of California. Protected by near-shore rocks, it has beckoned to people for thousands of years. Two Native American cultural groups, the Northern Chumash (Obispeño) and Playanos Salinan, utilized Point Piedras Blancas. The boundary between the two cultures is unresolved and may have shifted over time. Piedras Blancas was used primarily for marine and terrestrial resource gathering and stone tool-making. In the fall of 2005, archaeologists collected information about the earliest human visitors to Piedras Blancas. Radiocarbon dating of organic material yielded a date 3370–2,940 years before the present, although the site may have been used earlier. (Courtesy BLM Collection.)

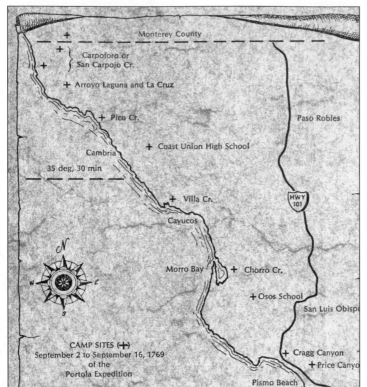

Spanish history in the area dates back to the Portola land expedition in 1769. Fr. Juan Crespi's journal refers to Playanos Salinans at what is now Arroyo de la Cruz, three miles north of Point Piedras Blancas. With the establishment of the mission system, Piedras Blancas fell under the jurisdiction of Mission San Miguel. (Map from *Captain Portola in San Luis Obispo County in 1769*, Tabula Rasa Press, 1984.)

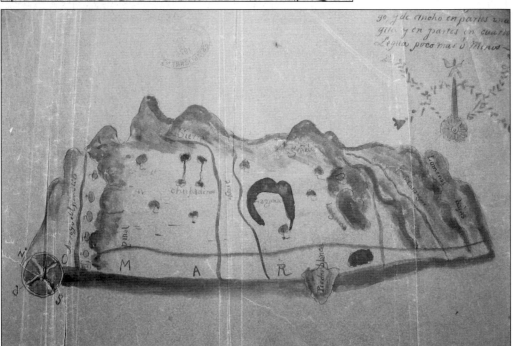

After secularization of the missions, Point Piedras Blancas was granted to Don Jose de Jesus Pico as part of the Mexican land grant Rancho Piedra Blanca. Above is the 1840 *diseño* (image) depicting the boundaries of Rancho Piedra Blanca. (Courtesy PBLS Collection.)

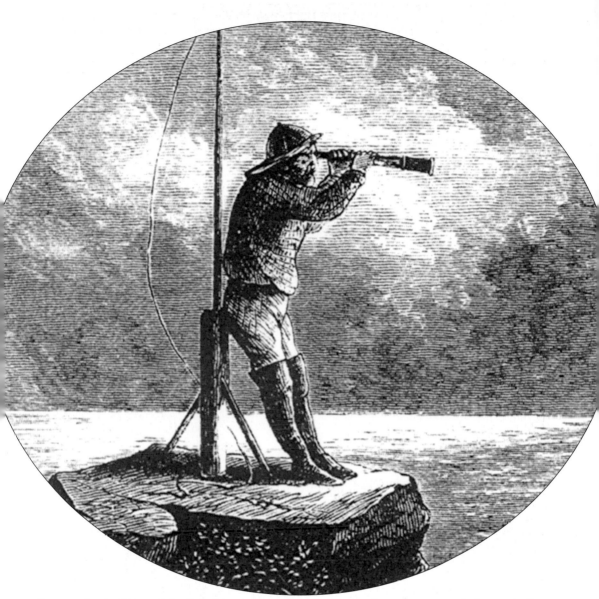

Prior to the building of the lighthouse, Capt. Joseph Clark, who ran a seasonal shore whaling station out of nearby San Simeon, is said to have maintained a lookout at Point Piedras Blancas during the southbound migration of the gray whale, their primary target. The San Simeon Whaling Station operated from 1864 to 1893. During the first 10 years, it was very successful, but after that, the numbers dropped. Whale oil was used for lubrication and illumination. However, whale oil was never used in lighting the first-order Fresnel lens at Piedras Blancas. Although sperm whale oil had been used by lighthouses in earlier years, by the time the Piedras Blancas lighthouse was established, it was too expensive to use. This illustration is of an unidentified location. However, the scenario would have been the same: a lookout with a spyglass and a flagpole to use in signaling the whaling ships. (Courtesy *Harper's Weekly*, 1877.)

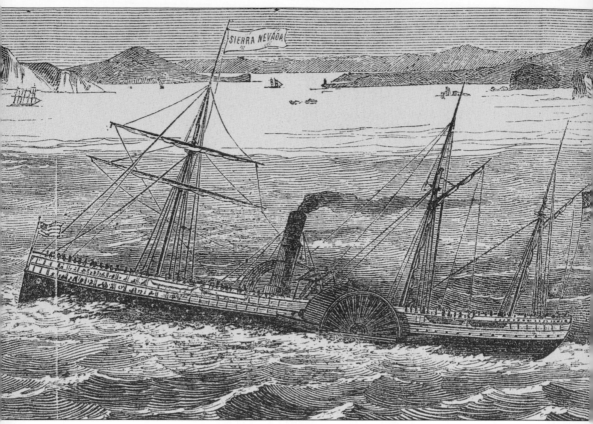

In 1869, two shipwrecks occurred that highlighted the need for a lighthouse in the Piedras Blancas area. An iron bark called the *Harlech Castle* struck a submerged rock about one and a half miles north of Point Piedras Blancas on August 29, 1869. Two crewmen drowned. The survivors were picked up by whalers from the San Simeon whaling station and returned to San Francisco aboard the steamer *Sierra Nevada*. On a foggy night in October of the same year, 1869, the *Sierra Nevada* struck a reef about three miles north of Point Piedras Blancas and wrecked. The passengers spent a harrowing night at sea in lifeboats before they could row to San Simeon in the morning. All 78 people were saved. There are two geographical features named after these shipwrecks: the Harlech Castle Rock and Point Sierra Nevada. The illustration above is of the *Sierra Nevada* passenger and cargo steamship. (Courtesy Robert V. Schwemmer Maritime Collection.)

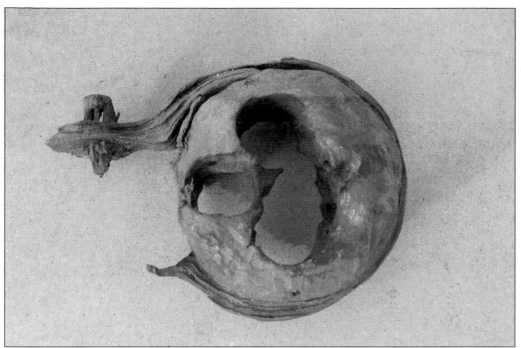

Artifacts from the Piedras Blancas collection include a dead-eye from the *Harlech Castle* (above). The collection also contains artifacts from the *Sierra Nevada*, including this brass porthole (below). The artifacts were donated by diver Bob Thomas, who collected them prior to the establishment of the Monterey Bay National Marine Sanctuary in 1992. Collection and possession of historic resources in the sanctuary is now prohibited. For more information, go to montereybay.noaa.gov. (Courtesy PBLS Collection.)

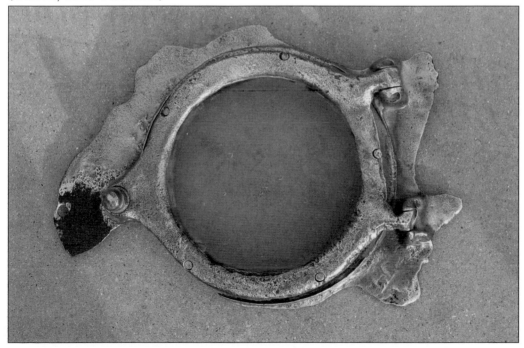

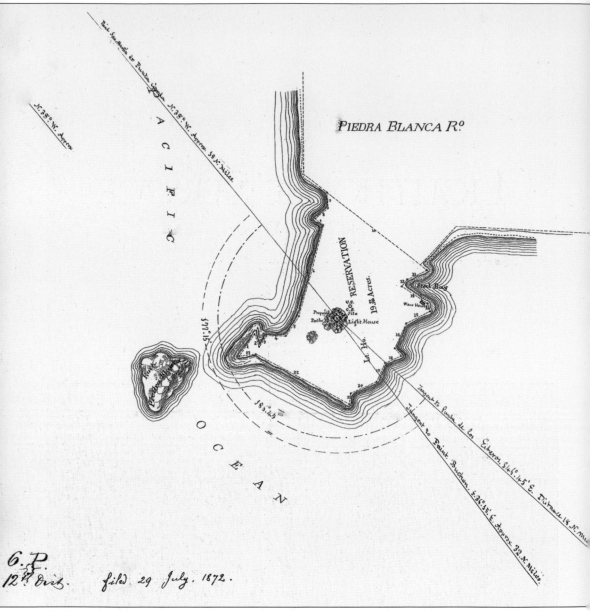

On June 18, 1866, Pres. Andrew Johnson signed the Lighthouse Reservation Act for the West Coast, which authorized the construction of 13 lighthouses, including Piedras Blancas. When Rancho Piedra Blanca was surveyed by the U.S. government in 1868, the portion embracing Point Piedras Blancas was owned by Juan Castro, who wanted to keep the point as part of the rancho. Surveys conducted in 1870, 1872, and 1873 confirmed Piedras Blancas as the logical site for a "first order" lighthouse, and the federal government ultimately selected Piedras Blancas. (Courtesy PBLS Collection.)

Two

LIGHTHOUSE SERVICE
1875–1939

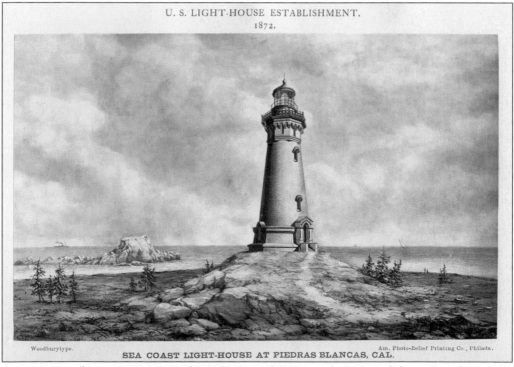

An artist's rendition appearing in the 1872 *Annual Report to the U.S. Lighthouse Board* gives the first glimpse of the proposed Piedras Blancas Lighthouse. (Courtesy PBLS Collection.)

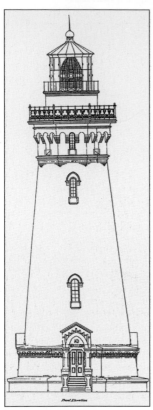

An appropriation of $75,000 was approved on June 10, 1872, for the construction of a first-order light and fog signal at Piedras Blancas. Material for the brick-and-steel tower was shipped from San Francisco on the *San Luis* and was brought ashore at the beach south of the point on April 25, 1874. The tower was constructed by the U.S. Corps of Engineers under the supervision of Captain Ashley. A crew of 25–35 men completed the lighthouse in less than 10 months. The light was first lit on February 15, 1875. Below is an earlier proposed version of the Piedras Blancas Lighthouse that was more Gothic in appearance than the elegant design that was chosen. (Courtesy PBLS Collection.)

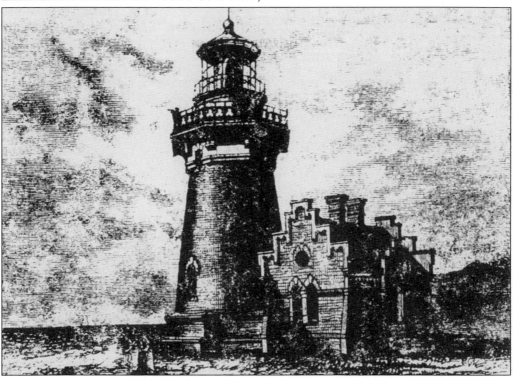

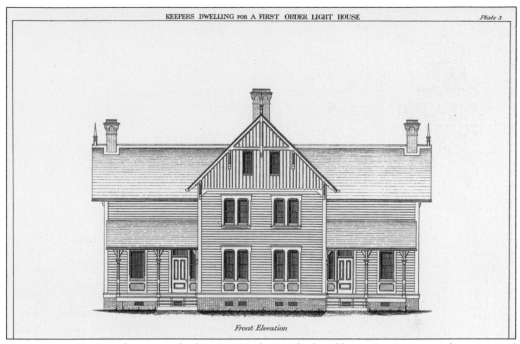

Front Elevation

A two-story Victorian house was built in 1876 to house the head keeper, two assistant keepers, and their families. The house was designed as a duplex but was used by three families, so conditions were crowded and sometimes led to unhappiness and strife. The attic was used for storage. While the house was being built, the keepers lived in crude shanties along the northwest bluff that were built to house the construction workmen. (Courtesy PBLS Collection.)

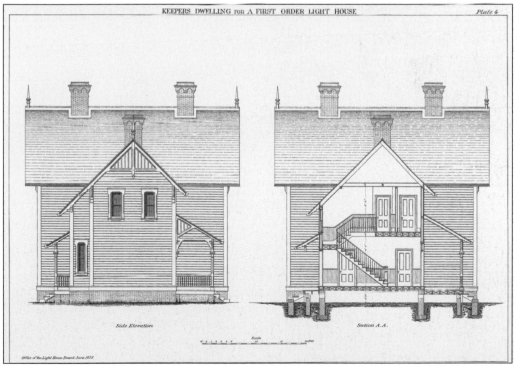

Side Elevation   *Section A.A.*

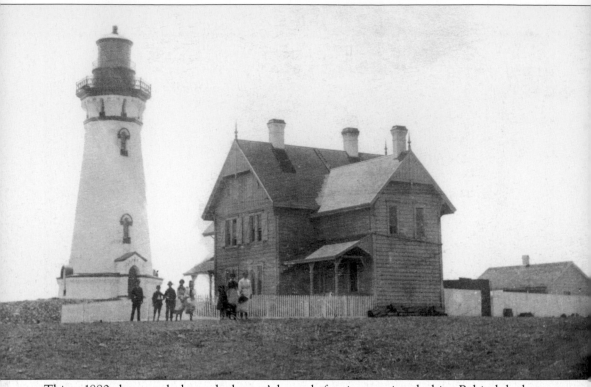

This *c.* 1880 photograph shows the keeper's house before it was painted white. Behind the house is a storeroom where supplies, including coal for the cooking stoves, were kept. A fence surrounds the area between the house and storage building. The site looks desolate despite the attractive structures and picket fence. (Courtesy PBLS Collection.)

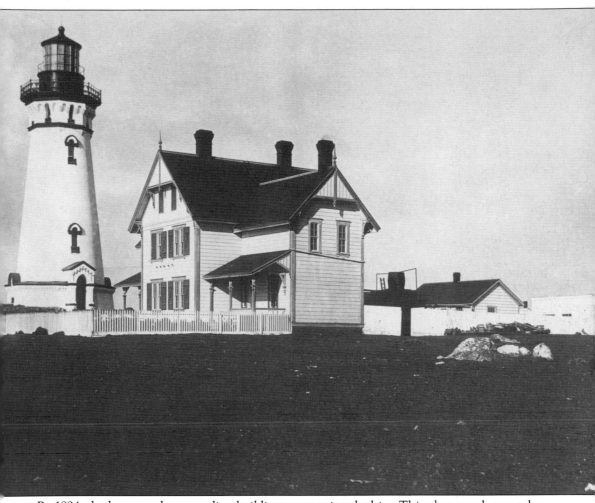

By 1894, the house and surrounding buildings were painted white. This photograph was taken as part of a series by Herbert Bamber in 1894. (Courtesy PBLS Collection.)

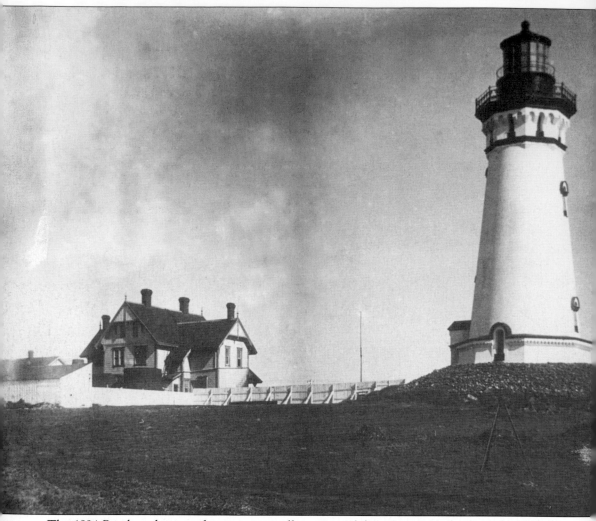

The 1894 Bamber photographs give an excellent view of the structures present at the Piedras Blancas Light Station at that time. There was a wind fence between the house and tower, and all the structures are gleaming white. (Courtesy PBLS Collection.)

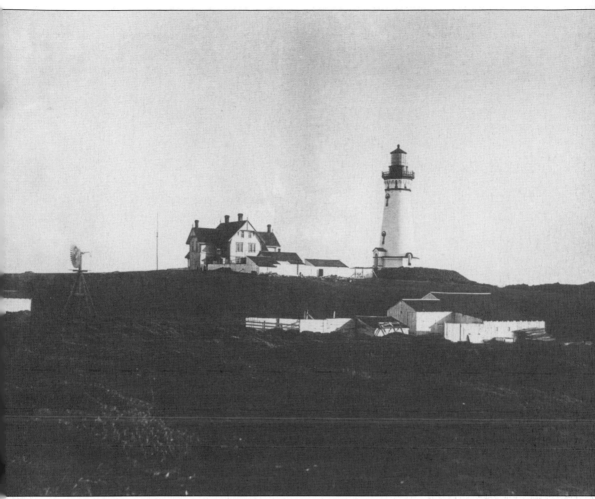

Another of the Bamber images from 1894 shows the outbuildings, including a corral, barn, and sheds. The windmill on the left was used to pump water. Obtaining water has always been a problem at Point Piedras Blancas. The proximity of the windmill to the corral resulted in unhealthy drinking water. During a particularly bad drought year, drinking water had to be brought in by wagon from San Luis Obispo. (Courtesy PBLS Collection.)

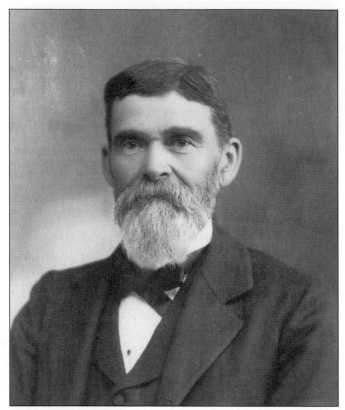

Lorin V. Thorndyke was the second head keeper at the Piedras Blancas Light Station. He held that position for 27 years, from August 19, 1879, until August 22, 1906, the longest term of service for any keeper at Piedras Blancas. Thorndyke was known as Captain Thorndyke because he had been a merchant seaman for many years. He claimed to have been around the world five times. Thorndyke was born in West Camden, Maine, on January 28, 1839. After joining the lighthouse service, he worked at several California lighthouses, including Santa Cruz, Half Moon Bay, San Francisco, and Point Hueneme, before becoming head keeper at the Piedras Blancas Light Station. (Courtesy Donna Jean Schneider.)

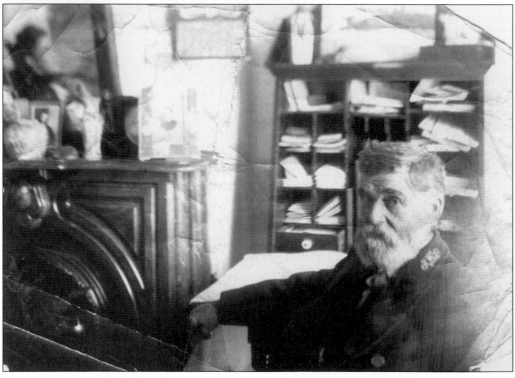

Captain Thorndyke married Elizabeth Jarmon in 1879. Lizzy, as she was called, was 27 years old at the time of their marriage. They had two sons. Lorin V. Thorndyke Jr. was born in 1881. John Emory Thorndyke was born in 1882. Elizabeth died in 1886. (Courtesy Donna Jean Schneider.)

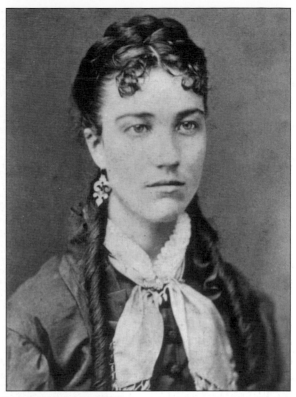

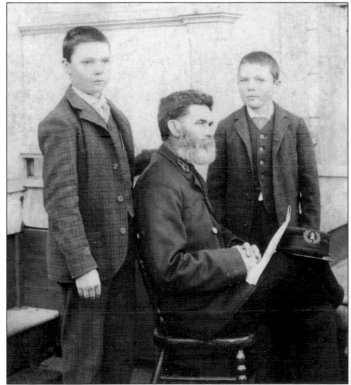

Captain Thorndyke is seen here with his two sons, L. V. Jr. (left), known as "Lo," and John Emory (right), known as "Em." Both boys went to school at the Washington School, about two miles north of Piedras Blancas. (Courtesy Donna Jean Schneider.)

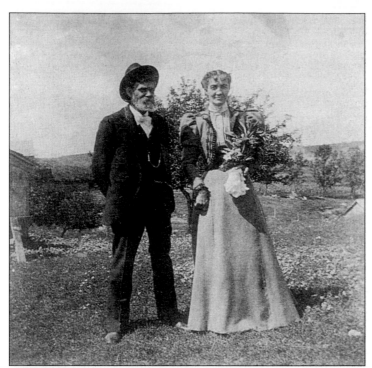

After Elizabeth died, the captain married a woman named Frank E. Clark, who bore him a daughter in 1891. Shortly after the daughter's birth, both mother and child moved to San Francisco. The captain married his third wife, Margaret L. Jarmon, in 1897. Margaret was the younger sister of his first wife, Elizabeth. The photograph at left is believed to be Margaret and the captain on their wedding day. (Courtesy Donna Jean Schneider.)

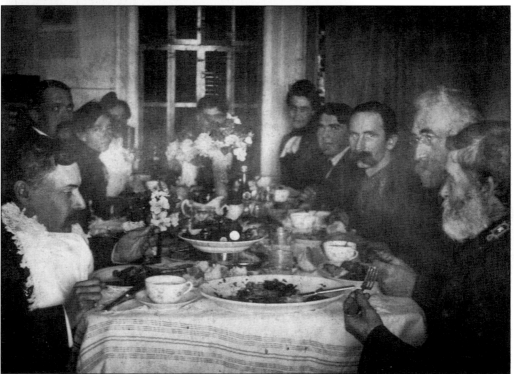

Captain Thorndyke is seated at the far right of this photograph. Margaret is sitting at the opposite end of the same row. Lorin Thorndyke Jr. is to the right of Margaret, and John Emory Thorndyke is to the left of Margaret behind the flowers. (Courtesy Donna Jean Schneider.)

Both Thorndyke sons spent time working for the lighthouse service. Lorin Jr. served at a lighthouse on San Francisco Bay. After becoming ill, Lorin Jr. took time off to recover his health while working for a cousin in Arizona. John Emory served as third assistant keeper at the Piedras Blancas Light Station from 1903 to 1906. This photograph is of Lorin Jr. (Courtesy Donna Jean Schneider.)

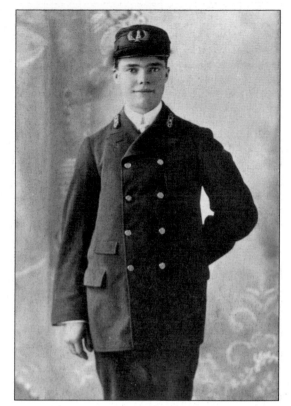

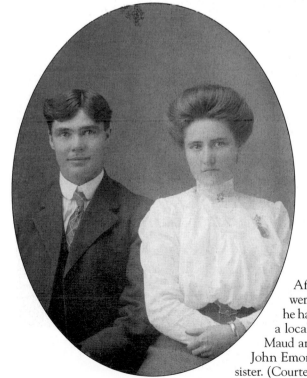

After Loren Jr. returned to California, he went to work for his father at the general store he had acquired in San Simeon. Loren married a local girl, Catherine Maud Rogers, in 1908. Maud and Lo are pictured here. Loren's brother, John Emory, married Clara Erma Rogers, Maud's sister. (Courtesy Donna Jean Schneider.)

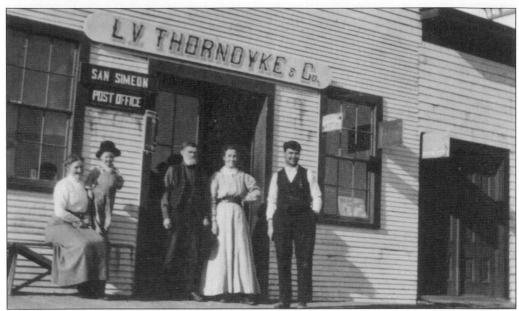

Pictured in front of the Thorndyke Store in San Simeon are three generations of Thorndykes. From left to right are Maud; her son, Roger; Captain Thorndyke; Margaret; and Loren Jr. After Captain Thorndyke retired from the lighthouse service, at age 75, he and Margaret moved into a small cottage behind the store. In 1914, the store was sold to Manual Sebastian and is known today as Sebastian's Store. (Courtesy Donna Jean Schneider.)

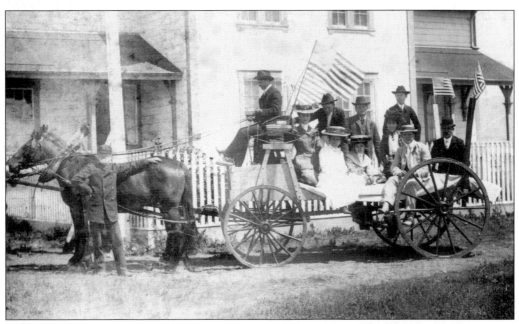

A wagon full of partygoers prepares to leave the light station. The flags and attire suggest they may be headed for the annual Fourth of July parade and festivities in Cambria. (Courtesy Donna Jean Schneider.)

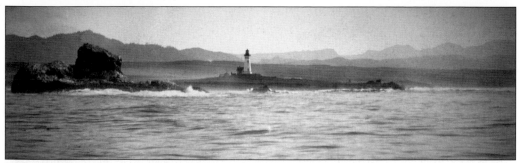

The Piedras Blancas Light Station as seen from the sea is beautifully captured in this image, taken before the fog signal building was constructed in 1906. Although there were plans to build a fog signal building at the time the lighthouse was constructed, it was delayed for several years because the funding was used to blast the hard foundation rock at the base of the tower. (Courtesy PBLS Collection.)

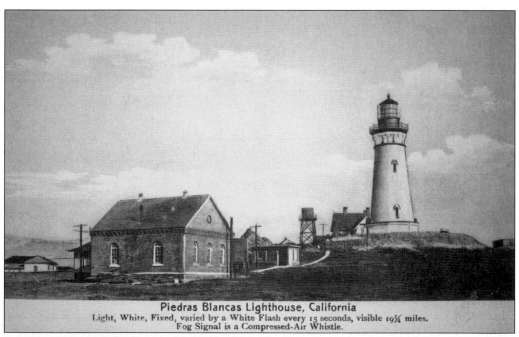

Piedras Blancas Lighthouse, California
Light, White, Fixed, varied by a White Flash every 15 seconds, visible 19¼ miles.
Fog Signal is a Compressed-Air Whistle.

A brick fog signal building was erected in 1906. The first sound signal was a whistle. This c. 1910 postcard shows all the major structures comprising the Piedras Blancas Light Station, including the fuel oil house, also built around 1906. This image shows the fog signal building before it was painted white. (Courtesy PBLS Collection.)

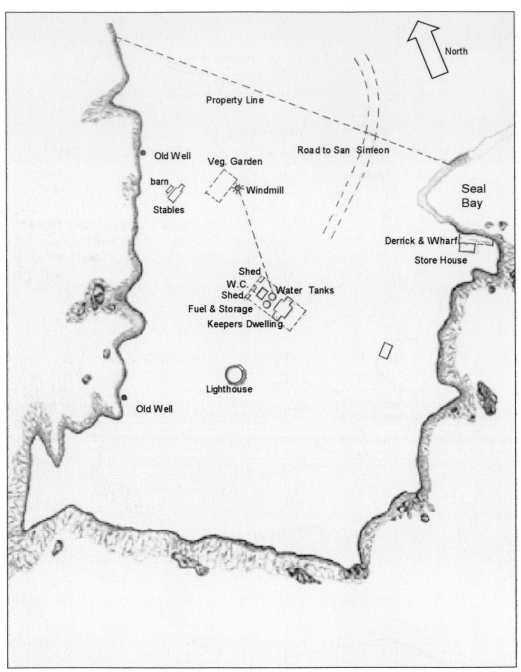

This map shows buildings and features present in 1880. The wells illustrated on the west side of the point may have been sunk by the original construction crew. No vestige of these wells remains today, and it is thought that these wells did not yield potable water—a common problem that existed throughout the lighthouse era. Also illustrated are the original barn, stables, windmill, and garden. A visit in 1910 by a naval engineer noted that all station personnel were ill. He deduced that it was most likely the water supply, which was probably contaminated by the close proximity of the stables and nearby garden. Station supplies were delivered periodically to the light station by tender and off-loaded at the wharf. (Map by Jerry Praver.)

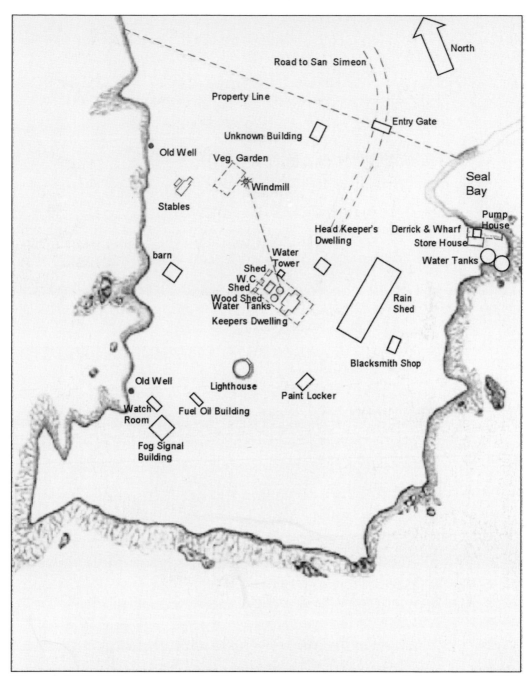

North

Road to San Simeon

Property Line

Entry Gate

Unknown Building

Seal
Bay

Old Well

Veg. Garden

Windmill

Pump
House

Stables

Head Keeper's
Dwelling

Derrick & Wharf

Store House

Water Tanks

barn

Water
Tower

Shed

W.C.
Shed

Wood Shed

Water Tanks

Keepers Dwelling

Rain
Shed

Blacksmith Shop

Old Well

Lighthouse

Paint Locker

Watch
Room

Fuel Oil Building

Fog Signal
Building

Through 1906–1914, there was a building spurt, as seen in this map of the station in 1910. Important new structures included the fog signal building, fuel oil house, the barn, head keeper's dwelling, the rain catchment, and water storage system. (Map by Jerry Praver.)

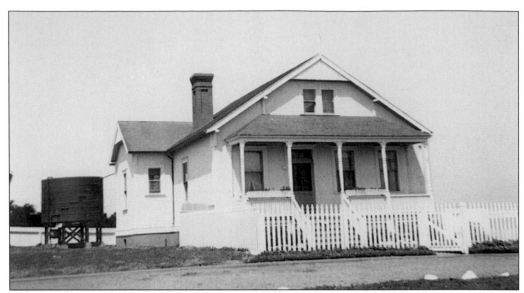

The addition of the fog signal equipment necessitated the hiring of a fourth keeper. Conditions in the duplex were already overcrowded, so a single head keeper's house was built just east of the two-story Victorian. (Courtesy PBLS Collection.)

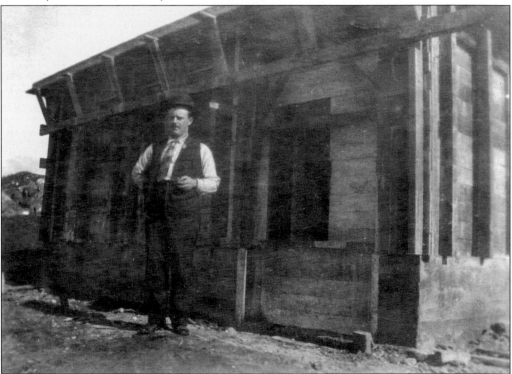

During 1906–1907, several building projects were undertaken. Shown here, under construction, is the fuel oil house used to store kerosene, which was too volatile to keep in the tower. The fuel oil house is listed on the National Register of Historic Places because it is one of the first reinforced concrete buildings constructed on the West Coast by the U.S. government. (Courtesy PBLS Collection.)

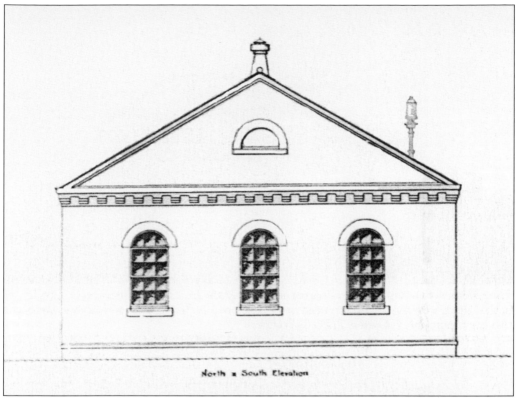

North x South Elevation

The fog signal building, built in 1906, is considered to be one of the most architecturally interesting sound-producing structures along the West Coast, if not the entire country. The original plans show the first signal used was a 10-inch whistle mounted on the back of the building. (Courtesy PBLS Collection.)

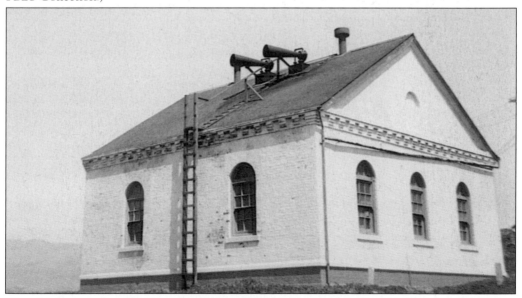

The whistle was replaced by a siren in 1912 and then by a two-toned diaphone and later by a diaphragm. Two large horns, mounted on the roof, projected the sound. (Courtesy PBLS Collection.)

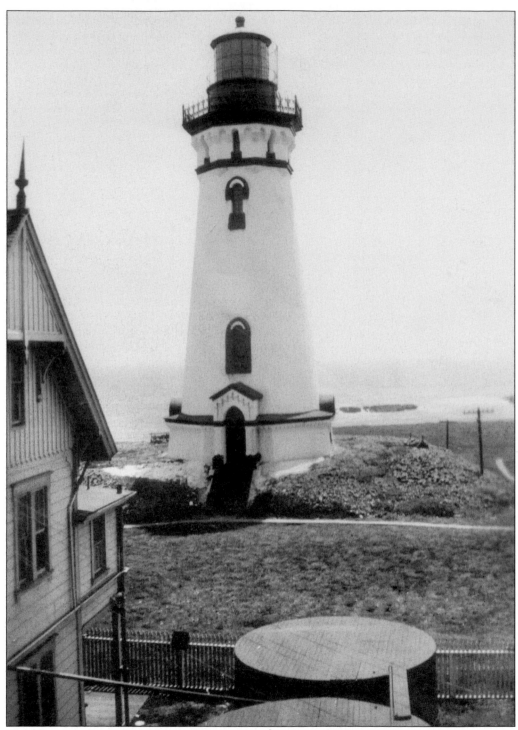

This photograph taken from atop a water storage tank located behind the keeper's house provides a beautiful view of the lighthouse. The poles on the north side of the lighthouse are part of the station intercom system, which linked the lighthouse, fog signal building, residences, and other outbuildings. (Courtesy PBLS Collection.)

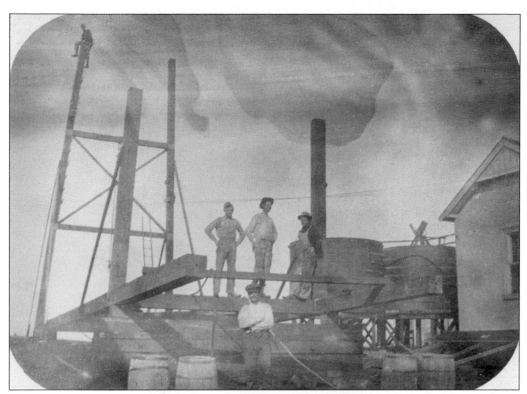

Workers pause during the construction of the water tower/storage system around 1910. Each of the tanks, supported by the tower, held 10,000 gallons. The tower was located on the footprint of the existing tank storage building, which still provides water storage for the site today. The tower was removed in 1935 when the existing water catchment and storage system was replaced by a spring-fed water source located one half mile northeast of the light station. (Courtesy PBLS Collection/Bogacki.)

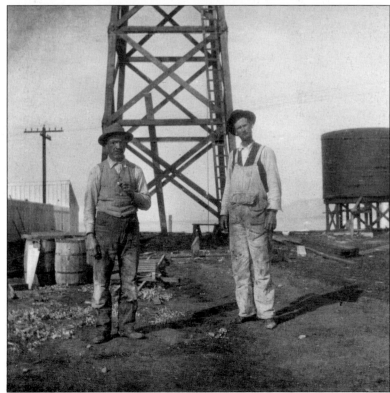

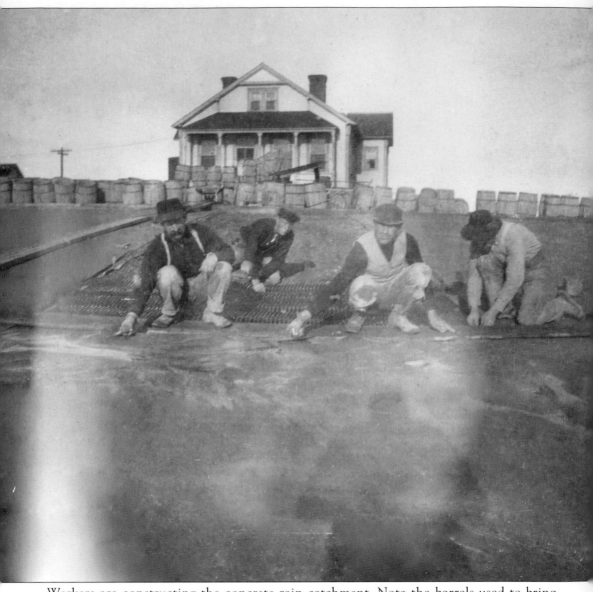

Workers are constructing the concrete rain catchment. Note the barrels used to bring Portland cement onto the site. In the background is the head keeper's house. (Courtesy PBLS Collection/Bogacki.)

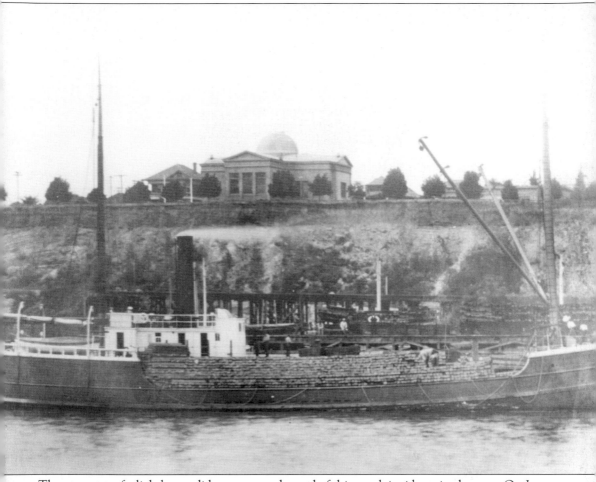

The presence of a lighthouse did not ensure the end of shipwreck incidents in the area. On June 6, 1913, the *Casco*, a commercial steam-driven schooner, struck a submerged rock about one and a half miles north of Point Piedras Blancas during a strong wind with clear skies. All 19 people on board survived. Above, the *Casco* is pictured at San Pedro Harbor. (Courtesy Maritime Museum of Monterey.)

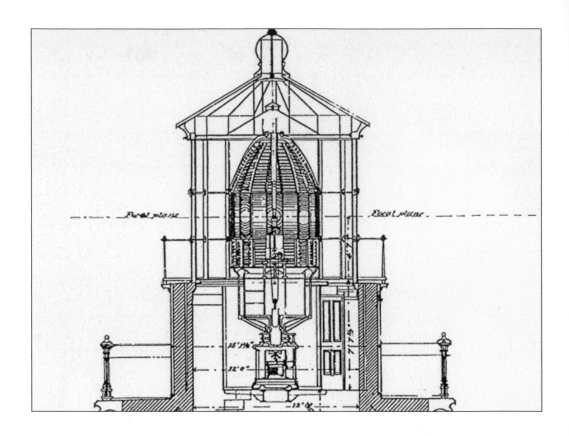

The first-order Fresnel lens used at Piedras Blancas was fixed and flashing until 1916. The horizontal prisms and lens would have created the "fixed" part of the signature. The curved prisms and lens created the "bull's-eye" (or flash) part of the signature. The light pattern that was created was a single flash every 15 seconds with a sheet of light of lesser intensity seen between flashes. The drawing below is not of the Piedras Blancas lens but it is of similar configuration, with horizontal lenses alternating between the bull's-eye lenses. (Courtesy PBLS Collection/Adams.)

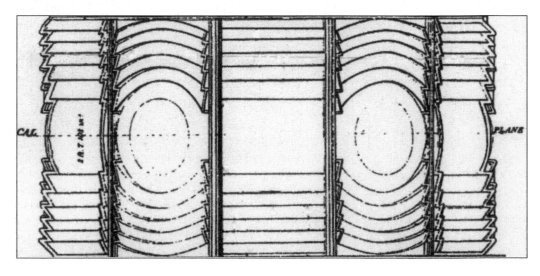

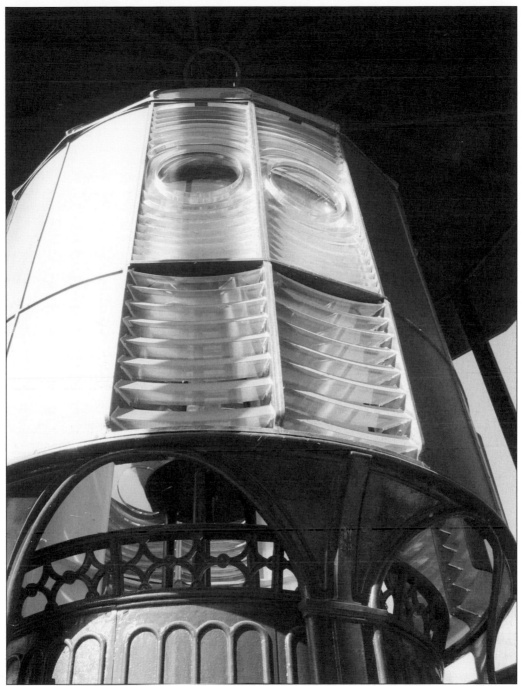

In 1916, the bull's-eye panels were repositioned in pairs so there are four sets of two sitting side-by-side. Opaque panels were introduced between the pair of bull's-eyes. This created a double flash with a period of darkness between flashes. The timing was adjusted so there were two flashes every 15 seconds. (Courtesy PBLS Collection/Adams.)

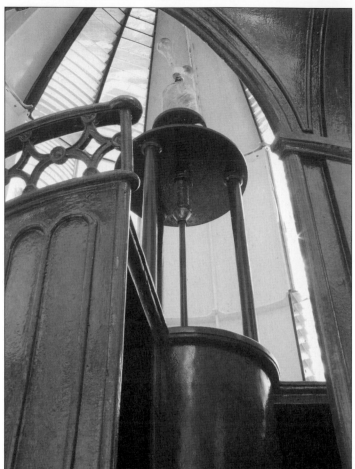

Steps inside the lantern led to the work platform on which the lamp standard was positioned. The first illuminant was lard oil, later replaced by kerosene, and finally by electricity. This photograph shows an electrical unit (which may not be the original). The first unit used would have contained lard oil and wicks, carefully trimmed and lit by the keepers. (Courtesy PBLS Collection/Adams.)

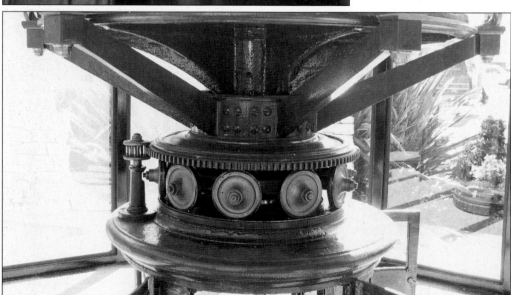

The base of the light rotated on chariot wheels. (Courtesy PBLS Collection/Adams.)

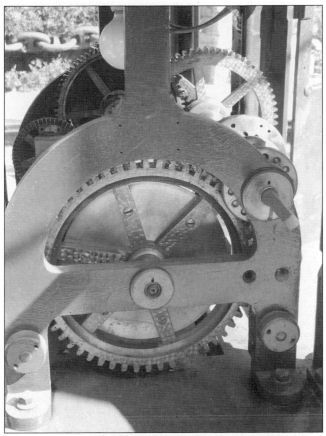

This mechanism is known as a clockwork because it worked much like a grandfather clock. An L-shaped crank fit onto the socket seen on the right of the upper photograph. It wound a 3/8-inch steel cable around the drum seen below. At the end of the cable (that extended all the way to the base of the tower) was a heavy weight. The cable was manually wound round the drum until the weight was suspended just below the first level deck. When released, the weight dropped, thereby actuating the mechanism that in turn rotated the light. (Courtesy PBLS Collection/Adams.)

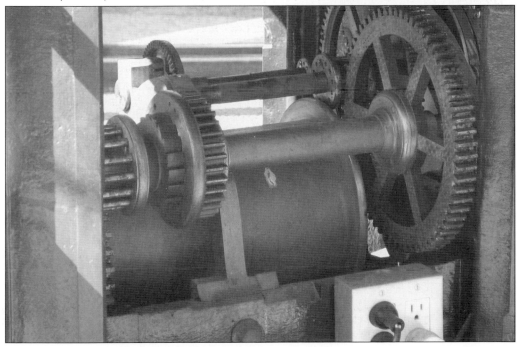

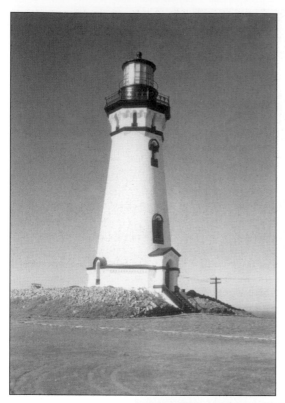

At the time the photograph at left was taken (around 1932), the lighthouse was beautifully maintained. However, a closer inspection would reveal the upper part had suffered damage during earthquakes dating back to the late 1800s. In the enlargement below, look closely to see two steel compression bands around the outside of the fourth floor landing, used to stabilize the upper portion of the tower. (Courtesy PBLS Collection.)

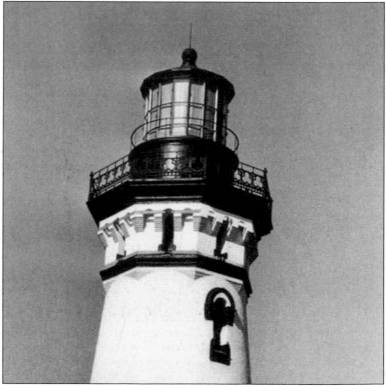

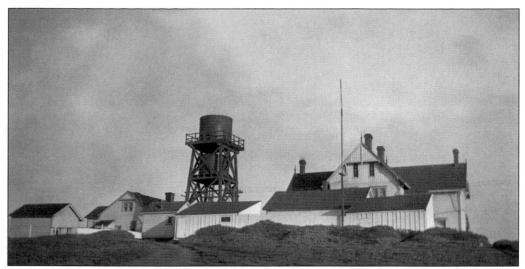

A view of the north side of the housing area shows the collection of storage rooms and sheds in place around 1930. The double-level water storage tanks held 10,000 gallons each. (Courtesy PBLS Collection/Inabnit/Mattson.)

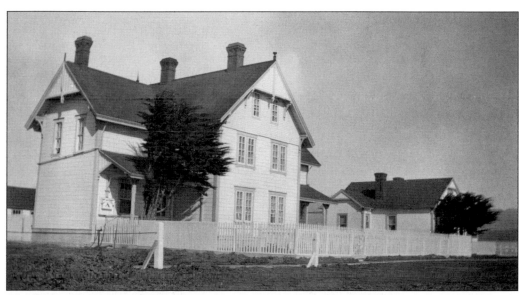

The front of the houses faced south, sheltering the entrances from the predominant northwesterly winds that scour the point on most days. The two-story Victorian house was used by three keepers, while the single-story house was used by the head keeper and his family. (Courtesy PBLS Collection.)

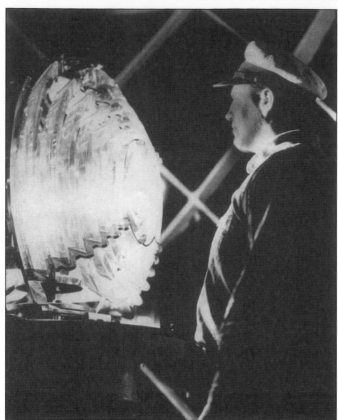

Norman Frances became head keeper at Piedras Blancas in 1934. His career began under the U.S. Lighthouse Service. He made the transition to U.S. Coast Guard and remained head keeper at the Piedras Blancas Light Station until 1947. He is shown here at the Los Angeles Harbor light, an assignment prior to Piedras Blancas. (Courtesy PBLS Collection.)

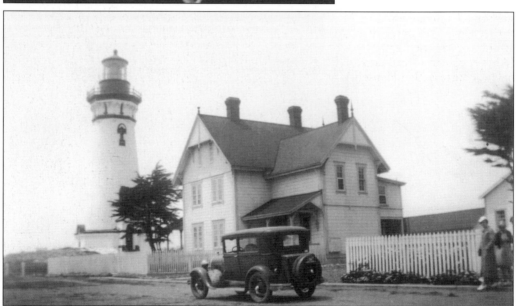

This photograph was probably taken in the early 1930s. The lighthouse is intact, although the upper portion had been structurally compromised by that time. The two-story Victorian house is seen behind a very tall fence. Notice the ladies pictured to the right of the photograph. (Courtesy PBLSA Collection/Mattson and Null.)

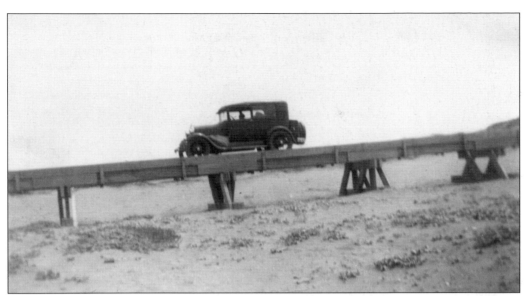

A large sand dune that stretched between Highway 1 and the light station was difficult for automobiles to cross, so a raised trestle was built. The tires had to remain precisely within the trough on the upper surface. This provided an exciting challenge, especially in foggy weather. There are anecdotal stories about children being afraid to cross the trestle. (Above, courtesy Jan Mattson; below, courtesy Neil Hansen.)

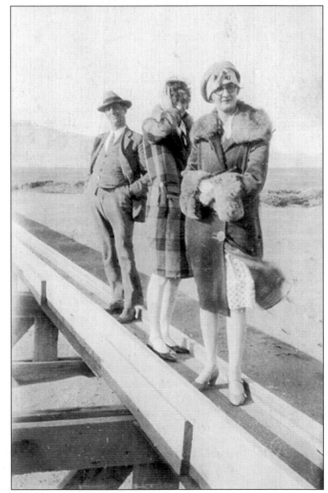

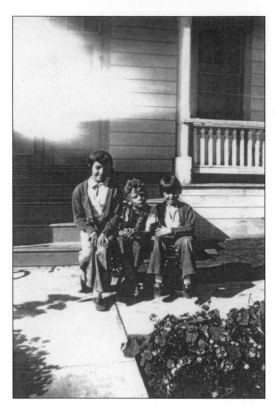

Agnes and Florence Gonzales are daughters of John Gonzales, third assistant keeper at Piedras Blancas from 1934 to 1937. The little boy in between them is Donald Mayeau. The Gonzales family welcomed a son, John, into the family when they lived at Piedras Blancas. In 2004, the children of John Gonzales Sr. donated their father's collection of lighthouse implements to the Piedras Blancas Light Station. (Courtesy PBLS Collection/Gonzales.)

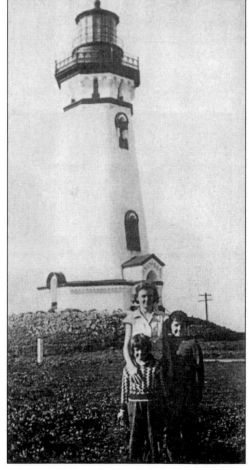

The Gonzales girls, Florence (left) and Agnes (right), are pictured here with Leonore Frances, daughter of head keeper Norman Frances, in 1939. One of the favorite anecdotes from that era refers to Leonore and her father, who used to sing opera inside the lighthouse because of the outstanding acoustics. Leonore was also skilled at playing piano. (Courtesy PBLS Collection.)

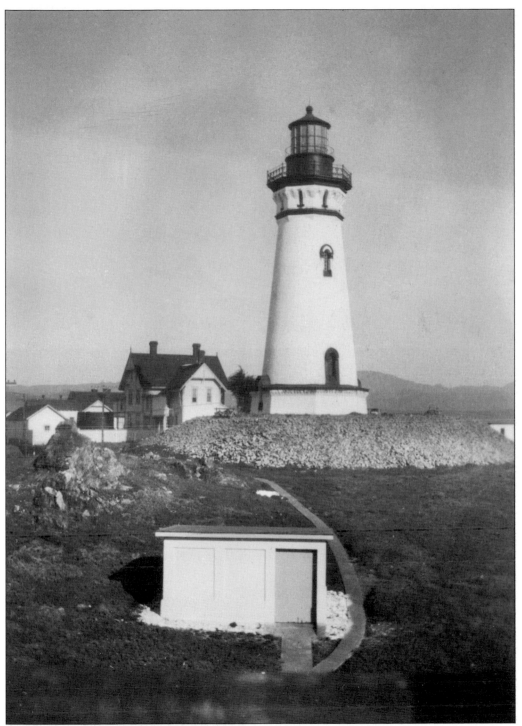

This unusual vantage point is from on top of the fog signal building. The fuel oil house appears to have just received a fresh coat of paint. Whitewash was used to paint the structures until sometime in the 1960s. Also visible on the far right is the paint locker, where all the paint and lubricants were stored. (Courtesy PBLS Collection.)

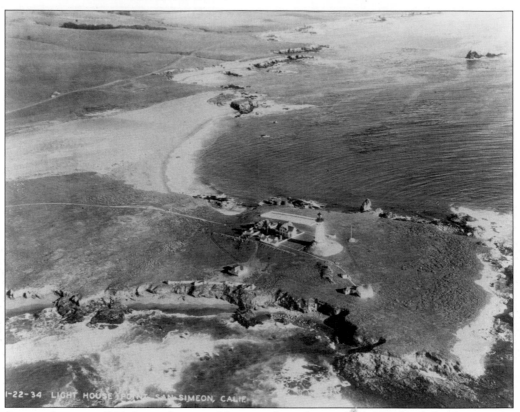

An aerial view in 1934 shows the row of shanties along the north bluff. Behind the shanties is a barn built around 1910. A concrete rain catchment is seen beyond the houses. Rainwater was gravity fed to two redwood storage tanks and was then pumped back up to the houses. The system was not effective because of inadequate rain and the presence of gulls! (Courtesy PBLS Collection.)

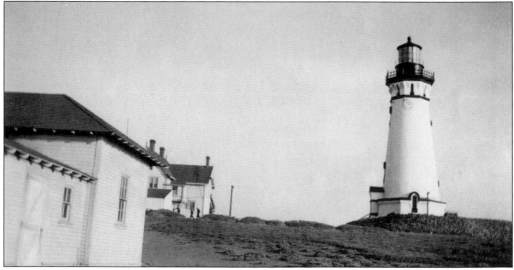

This view of the windswept area between the barn and the tower, around 1934, gives a first glimpse of the young cypress hedge planted along the sidewalk around 1932 as a windbreak. (Courtesy PBLS Collection/Mattson.)

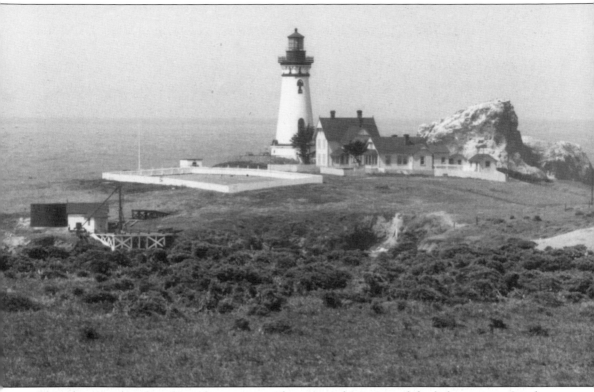

This photograph, taken from the east, provides a marvelous view of the light station. On the left is the wharf area. The rainwater catch basin is clearly seen, as are the tower, houses, and outbuildings. The young cypress hedge can be seen to the far right of the buildings. (Courtesy PBLS Collection/Mattson.)

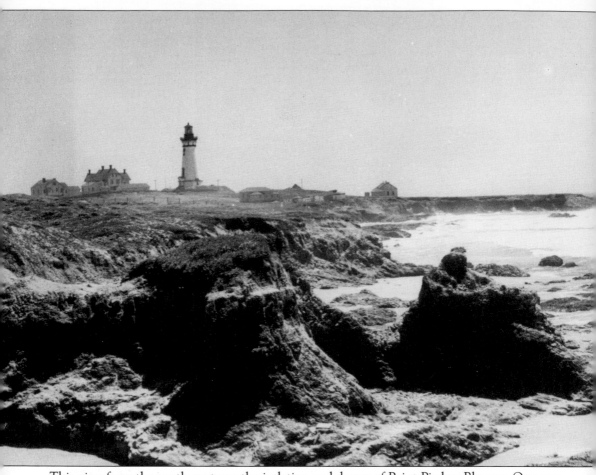

This view from the north captures the isolation and drama of Point Piedras Blancas. One can almost hear the wind! From left to right are the head keeper's house, the two-story Victorian house, the tower, the barn, the shanties along the bluff, and the fog signal building. (Courtesy PBLS Collection.)

Three

U.S. COAST GUARD
1939–2001

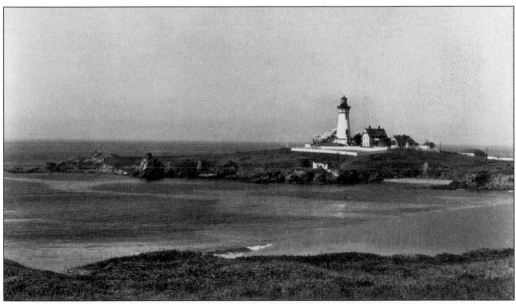

The U.S. Coast Guard assumed management of the Piedras Blancas Light Station in 1939. In the above photograph is the station as it appeared at that time. The wharf, storeroom, and water tanks are on the wind-protected side of the point, where the water is calm. Supplies were delivered by tender. On the upper level, the concrete water catch basin is in front of the houses. The tower is complete and well kept. The barn is visible on the right side of the photograph. (Courtesy PBLS Collection.)

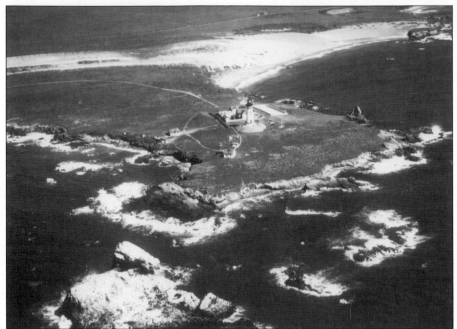

These aerial photographs depict the classic light station about the time the coast guard took over. Times were changing, and rapid advancements in technology would soon change the face of the station. Visible in the lower photograph is the concrete water catchment, which was converted to its highest and best use—as a basketball court! It was also a wonderful location to dry laundry. Picturesque Seal Cove often hosted volleyball, barbeques, and other social activities for station personnel. (Courtesy PBLS Collection.)

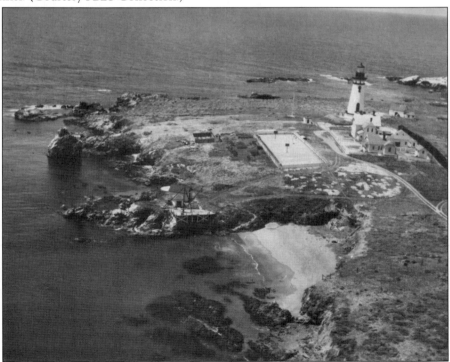

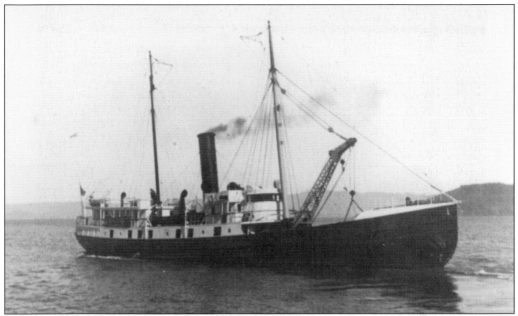

Tenders delivered supplies several times a year. Tenders during that era were named after native plants. Above is the *Sequoia*, which delivered supplies to Piedras Blancas. Two other tenders that delivered supplies along the West Coast were the *Armeria* (seen below) and the *Lupine*. Species of both of those native plants are found at Piedras Blancas. (Courtesy Monterey Museum of Maritime History.)

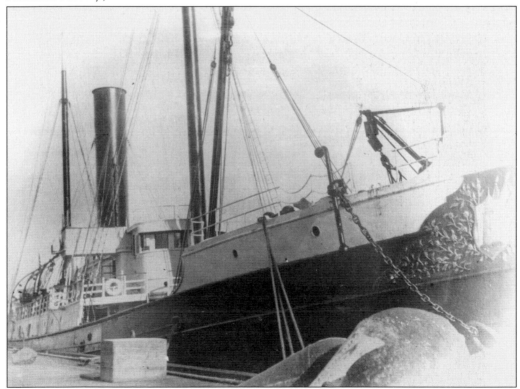

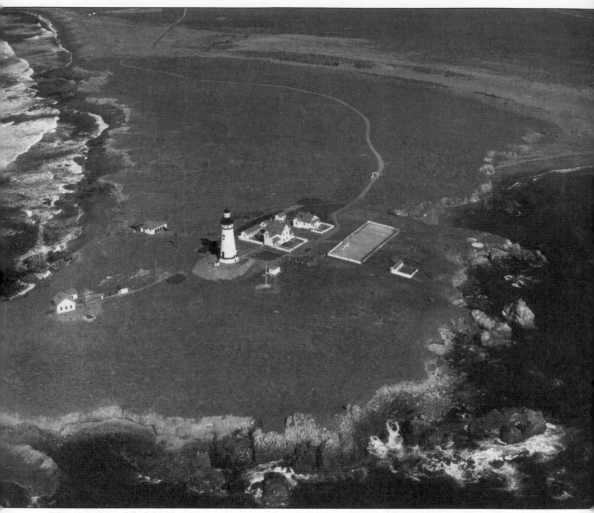

There is a wealth of information conveyed in this photograph taken around 1946. At the upper left, the original entry road to the station can be seen as it crosses the sand dune. It was over this area that the trestle was located. From there, the road swings south and winds in through the entry gate, arriving at the houses and lighthouse. A path leads from the lighthouse to the barn, which had been converted into a four-car garage. From the lighthouse to the fog signal building, at the lower left, there is a sidewalk, which also passes the fuel oil house and the watch room adjacent to the fog signal. The rocky base of the tower can be seen as well as the rocky mound to the south of the tower that supported a flagpole. White picket fencing surrounds the houses. To the right is the rain catchment. All of the structures associated with the wharf have been removed, leaving two concrete bases. The dark patches around the houses and along the sidewalk are patches of ice plant. The Piedras Blancas Light Station was poised on the brink of major change at the time this photograph was taken. (Courtesy PBLS Collection.)

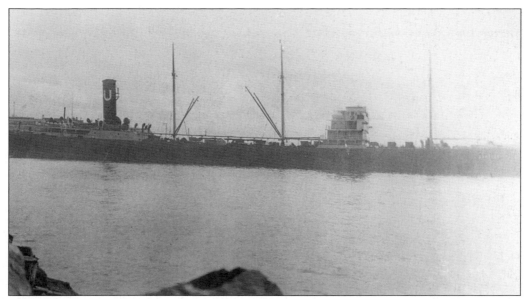

On December 23, 1941, the Union Oil tanker *Montebello* was torpedoed by the Japanese submarine I-21 and sank six miles off the south end of Cambria. She was carrying over three million gallons of crude oil. Norman Frances was called upon to be an official government witness in a legal case brought by Union Oil against the federal government to recover damages under the War Damage Act. (Courtesy Monterey Museum of Maritime History.)

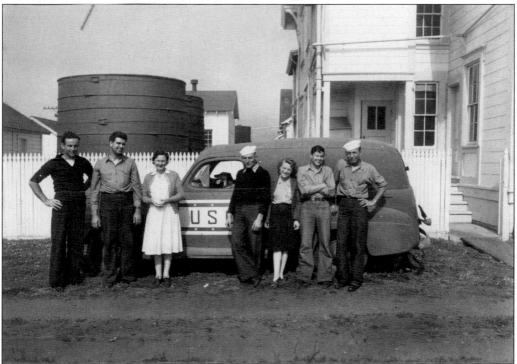

The men depicted in this photograph were assigned to Piedras Blancas in the postwar years, around 1948. The unidentified women were most likely wives of coast guard personnel. (Courtesy PBLS/Inabnit.)

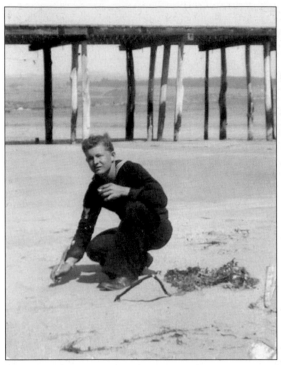

This is an unidentified coast guardsman stationed at Piedras Blancas during the 1940s. The photograph was taken at the San Simeon pier. (Courtesy PBLS Collection/Sewell.)

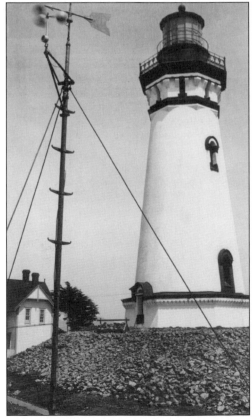

Another view of the tower, pre-1949, shows a weather station on the rocky outcropping along the sidewalk. (Courtesy PBLS Collection.)

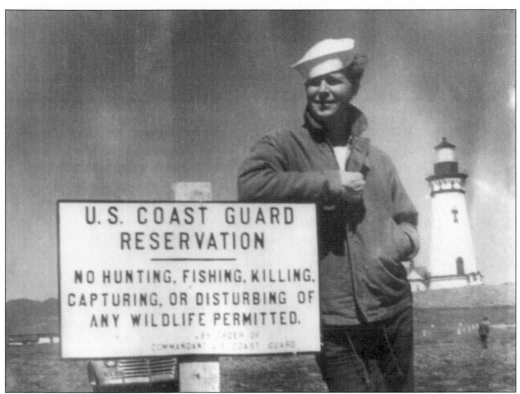

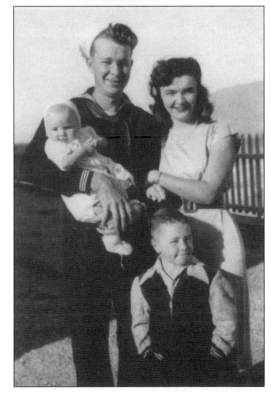

Bert Breedlove was officer-in-charge from 1949 to 1954. He was on duty in the fog signal building when the earthquake struck in December 1948 that caused the damage to the upper part of the tower and led to its being removed. (Courtesy PBLS Collection/Mattson.)

This photograph of the Bert Breedlove family is from a Christmas card sent to a friend stationed at Point Pinos Lighthouse. (Courtesy PBLS Collection/Mattson.)

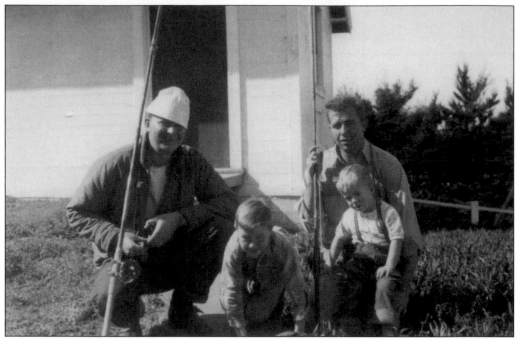

Bert Breedlove is pictured on the left as part of a fishing party. Fish was an important part of the diet of those stationed at Piedras Blancas. Part of the head keeper's storage building is showing in the background. (Courtesy PBLS Collection/Mattson.)

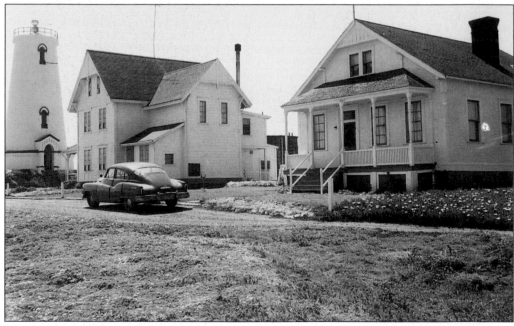

Due to structural damage, the upper part of the lighthouse was removed in 1949. The lighthouse was capped and a 36-inch aero beacon set in place. In this photograph, about 1950, the truncated lighthouse is seen on the left and a patch of ice plant is on the right. Ice plant was not only planted to stabilize areas that had been disturbed, it was also planted because it was considered to be an attractive, low-maintenance ground cover. (Courtesy PBLS Collection.)

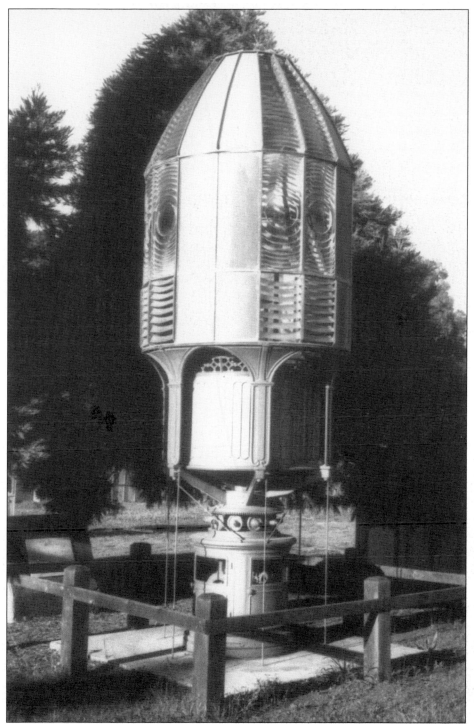

After the lens was removed from the tower in 1949, it was rescued by members of the Cambria Lions Club and taken to Cambria, where it is currently on display next to the Veteran's Memorial building. The above photograph was taken in 1986, before the protective housing was built around it. (Courtesy PBLS Collection/Adams.)

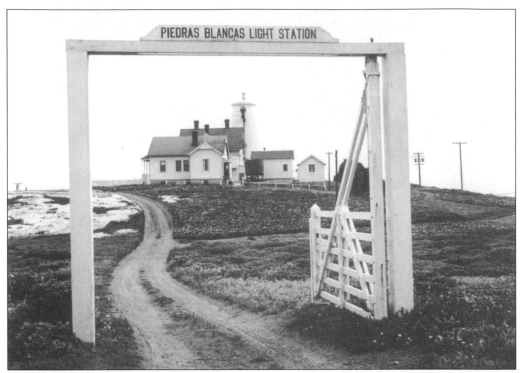

Two views of the light station taken in 1950 provide lovely glimpses of the station during that period. Guests entered through a gate that framed the houses and tower. The view from the south point shows native vegetation still dominates that area. (Courtesy PBLS Collection.)

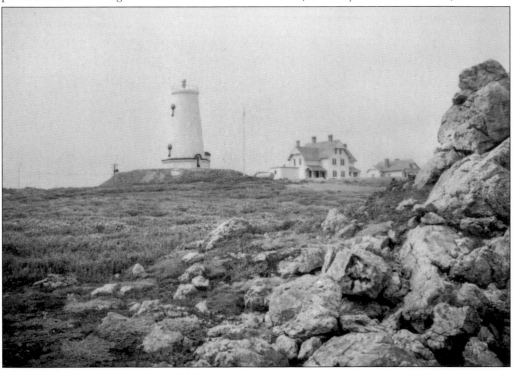

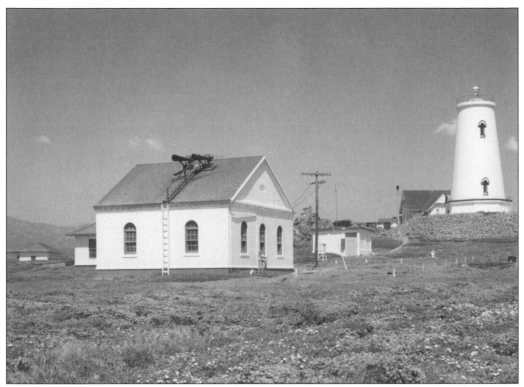

The buildings are gleaming white in this 1950 image. From the barn/garage at far left to the decapitated tower, everything appears well cared for. There is a preponderance of native plants in the foreground. (Courtesy PBLS Collection.)

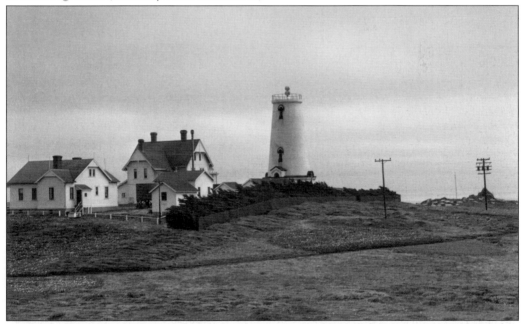

The entry road was rerouted in 1958 to come in past the garage and veer left, up to the houses. The cypress is protected by a wind fence. (Courtesy PBLS Collection.)

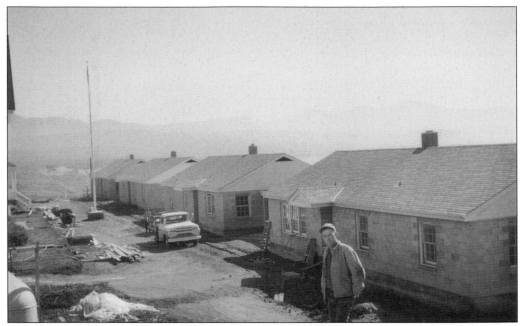

In 1960, construction began on a row of four block houses that were built to replace the aging Victorian houses. Known as "hurricane houses," they are a study in cookie-cutter quarters that were built by the coast guard at various other locations. The station personnel were eager to move into the more spacious, modern, comfortable, cockroach-free units. A forest of pine trees was planted where the houses had been and in front of the tower; however, they did not survive the harsh, windy conditions. (Courtesy PBLS Collection.)

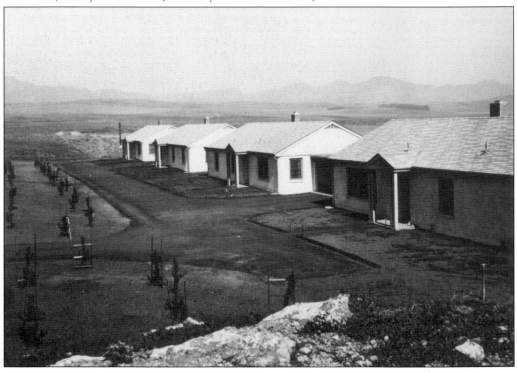

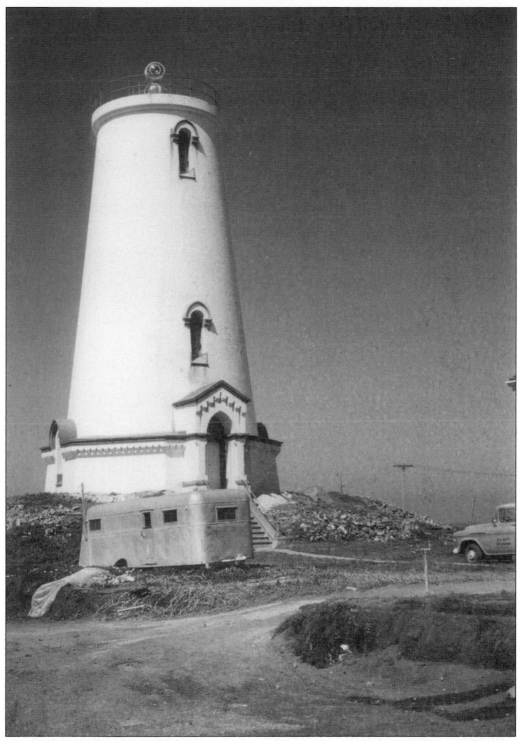

The upper lens of the 36-inch aero beacon on top of the tower seems to look over the construction of the houses like a giant eye. The trailer in front of the lighthouse was the contractor's field office. (Courtesy PBLS Collection.)

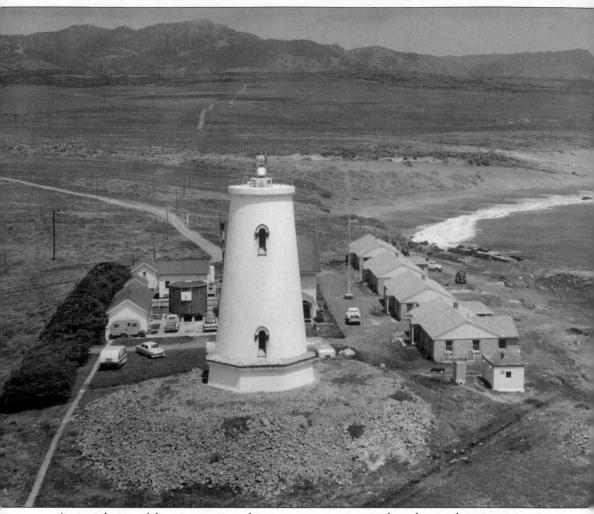

An aerial view of the construction phase captures a moment when the new housing units appear to be almost completed and the old two-story house is still standing. The paint locker is to the right, just south of the row of new houses. The cypress hedge is well maintained. The remnants of the original flagpole mound are visible on the right and the (then current) flagpole is positioned in front of the houses. The 36-inch aero beacon lens is vertically positioned to create a double flash every 15 seconds. (Courtesy PBLS Collection.)

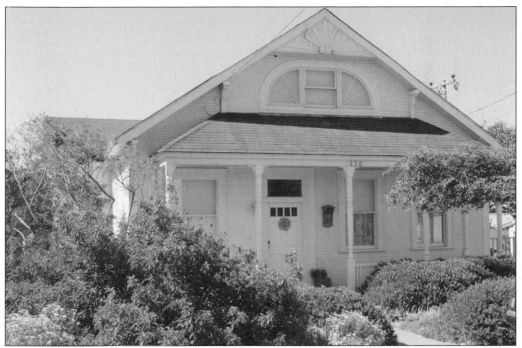

After the four new quarters were finished, the two-story Victorian was demolished and removed. The single-story head keeper's house was purchased for $1 and moved to Cambria in 1960. It has been restored and is now a vacation rental. (Courtesy PBLS Collection.)

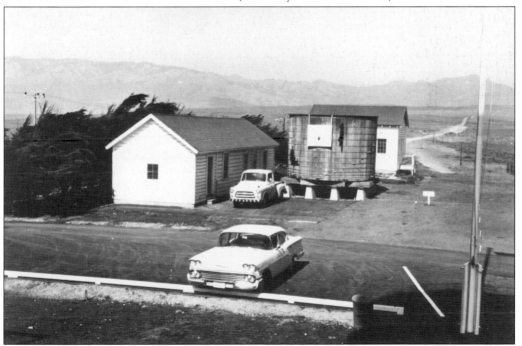

This 1960 photograph shows the old fuel and storage house, expanded on both sides in 1935 and now serving as the coast guard office. A new flagpole has been placed in front of the lighthouse. (Courtesy PBLS Collection.)

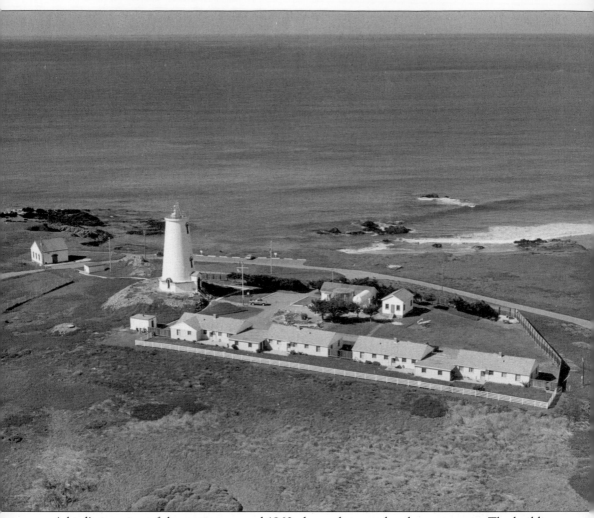

A bird's-eye view of the station, around 1960, shows the completed new quarters. The buildings are gleaming white, and a fence surrounds the housing units and support buildings. To the left of the houses is a paint locker. West of the paint locker is a rocky mound marking the original site of the flagpole. Prior to 1960, the buildings frequently received a fresh coat of whitewash. (Courtesy PBLS Collection.)

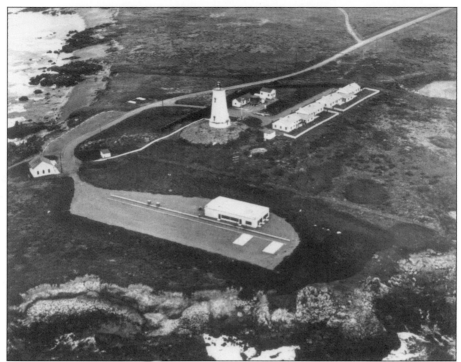

In 1959, construction began on a compound that was part of a proposed navy missile tracking station. However, the program was given to the U.S. Air Force, and the building was not completed. The photograph below shows the tremendous impact this latest building spurt had on the land. (Courtesy PBLS Collection.)

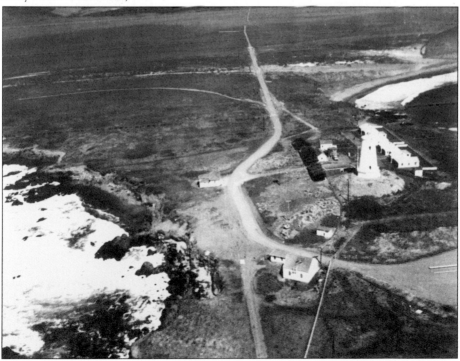

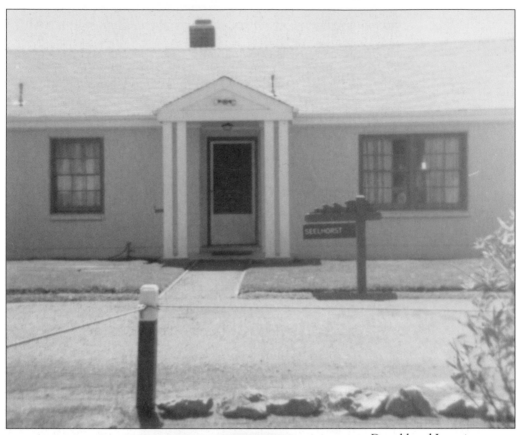

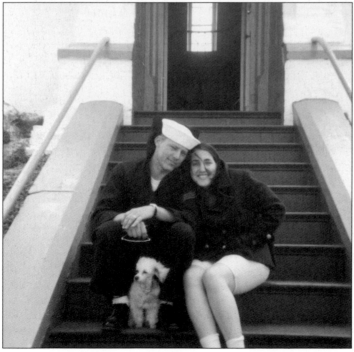

Donald and Lorraine Seelhorst, and their dog Reble (left), occupied quarters B (above) around 1973–1974. (Courtesy PBLS Collection/Seelhorst.)

A shield was placed on top of the tower to protect cars on the highway from the flashing light as it rotated past the eastern portion of the range. (Courtesy PBLS Collection.)

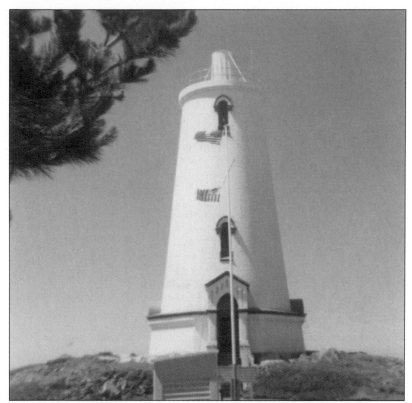

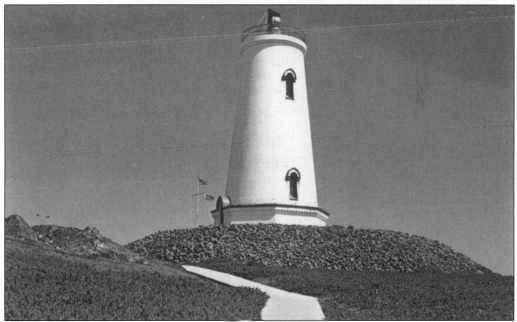

Ice plant was a solid ground cover west of the tower by the 1970s. The rocky base of the tower was covered over and planted with ice plant, too, just before the station became automated and unmanned. The last coast guardsman to be stationed at Piedras Blancas was Karl Johnson in 1975. (Courtesy PBLS Collection/Ruth.)

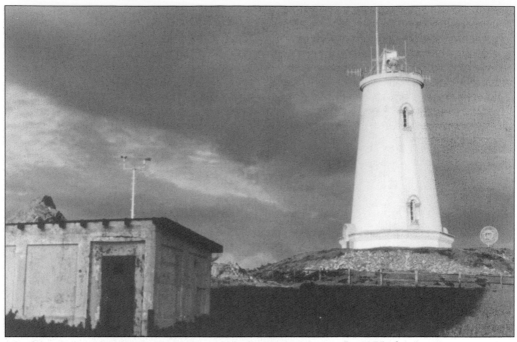

In 1975, the station was automated. A 24-inch aero beacon was placed on top of the tower. The light was joined by a myriad of communications antennae. With automation, it was no longer necessary to have personnel stationed at Piedras Blancas, and the site became unmanned. (Courtesy PBLS Collection/Wright.)

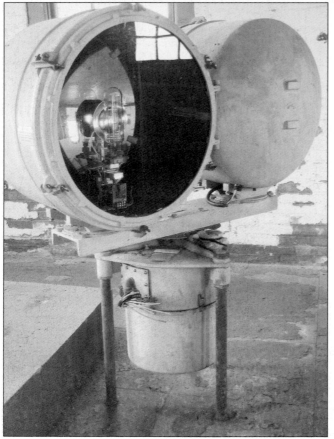

The 24-inch aero beacon rotated horizontally and produced a single flash every 10 seconds. One similar to it is currently on display at the Piedras Blancas Light Station. (Courtesy PBLS Collection.)

In 1993, Norman Frances Jr. and Marjorie Sewell visited the light station. He spent a lot of his childhood at the station because his father, Norman Frances Sr., was head keeper from 1934 to 1947. Marjorie, who grew up in San Simeon, used to play at the lighthouse as a child. Norman Jr. moved to Cambria at the end of his life to preserve the Fresnel lens on display in Cambria. (Courtesy PBLS Collection/Sewell.)

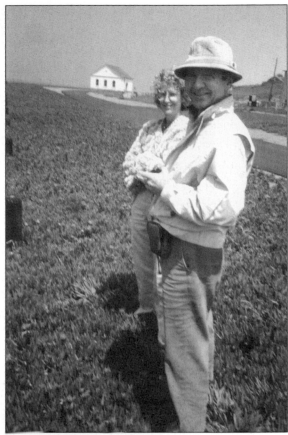

Norman Frances Jr. arranged to have the coast guard restore the lens and led the movement to build a secure enclosure to protect it. In 1990, the lens was taken to Monterey, where the cast-iron elements were refurbished by the coast guard. The brass and lens were restored by members of the Cambria Lions Club and the community. The protective glass lantern room was provided by the Friends of the Piedras Blancas Lighthouse Lens. (Courtesy PBLS Collection.)

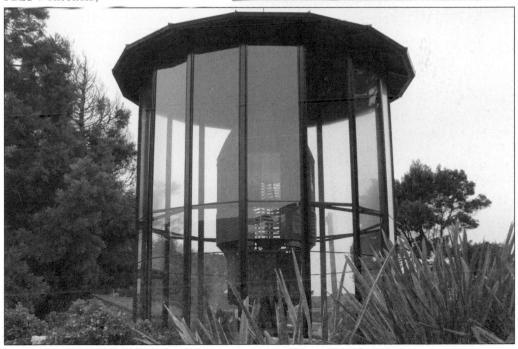

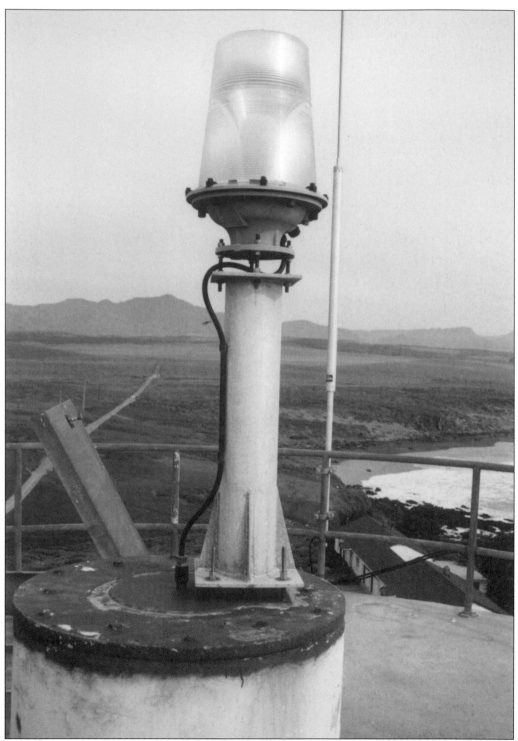

In 1999, the 24-inch aero beacon failed and could no longer be used. The emergency light was pressed into full-time service. The change was not favorably received by the citizens of Cambria, who complained the dim light could not be seen. (Courtesy PBLS Collection.)

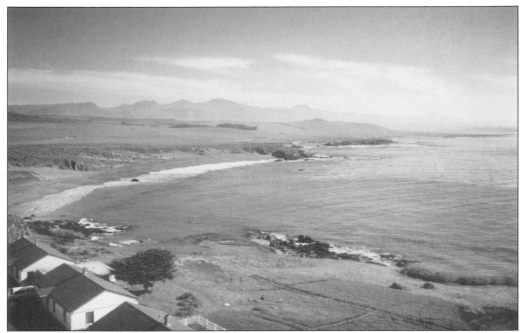

After the Piedras Blancas Light Station was automated in 1975, it was abandoned for a brief time. Ron Jameson, a biologist studying the recovery of the California sea otter, applied for and received permission from the U.S. Coast Guard to establish a biological research station at Point Piedras Blancas. In 1977, biologists occupied the site. The above photograph was taken in 1985. (Courtesy PBLS Collection.)

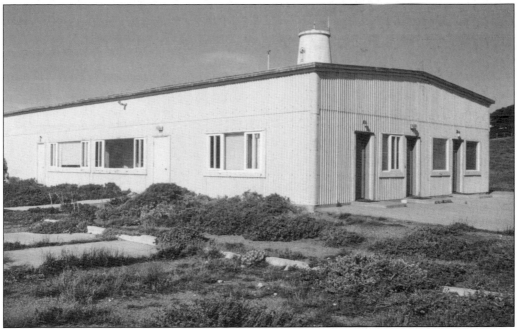

In 1960, the U.S. Navy built this temporary structure as a mobile instrumentation station to be used as part of a missile tracking facility. It was abandoned before completion. Biologists finished the office space and utilized it as a laboratory and office. (Courtesy PBLS Collection.)

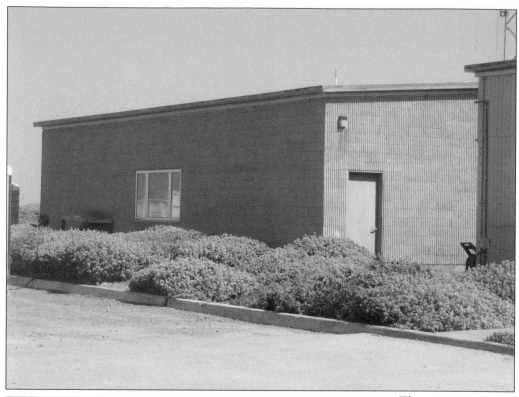

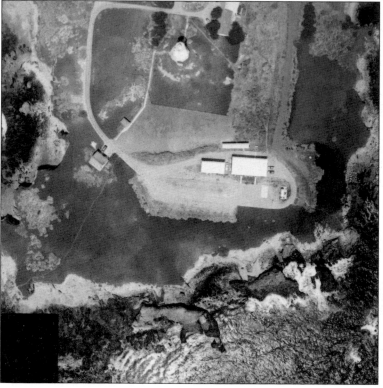

The garage next to the office was constructed by the biologists for use as boat and vehicle storage (above). The aerial photograph (left) was taken by Morgan Lynn, National Marine Fisheries Service biologist, in 1997. The three rectangular structures on the right are the garage and office, with a mobile office unit behind them. (Courtesy PBLS Collection/Lynn.)

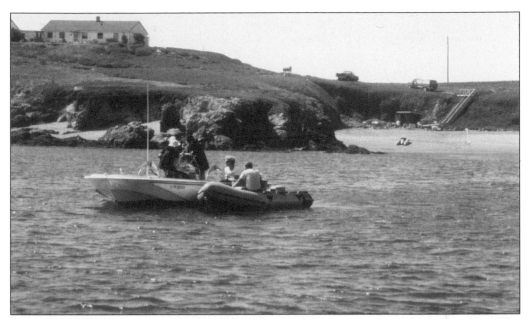

The primary area of study at the Piedras Blancas Research Station was the California sea otter. The sea otter translocation project was headquartered out of Piedras Blancas. Otters were captured along the central coast and moved to San Nicolas Island so there would be a portion of the population protected in case of an oil spill along the coast. (Courtesy PBLS Collection/Hatfield.)

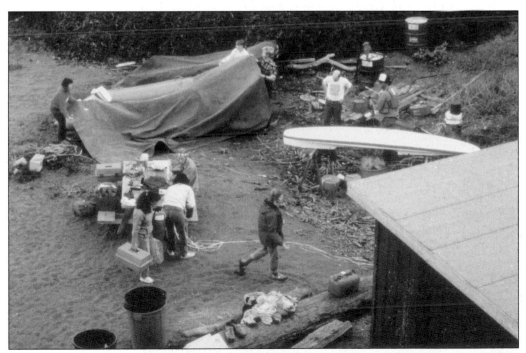

Seal Cove, referred to as Launch Cove by the biologists, was used as a center of operations when the team worked off Point Piedras Blancas. (Courtesy PBLS Collection/Hatfield.)

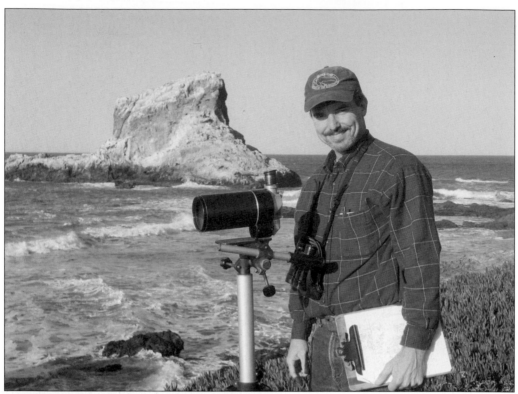

U.S. Geological Survey continues to do sea otter research at Piedras Blancas. USGS wildlife biologist Brian Hatfield conducted research at the light station for over 20 years. (Courtesy PBLS Collection.)

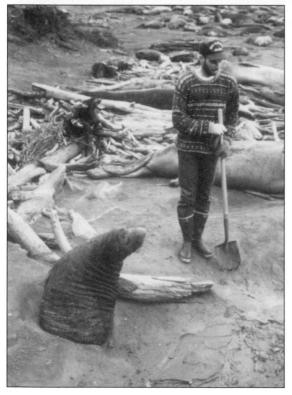

When elephant seals began using the beaches next to Piedras Blancas in 1990, the biologists found a new subject literally at their doorsteps. Occasionally elephant seals would make their way up to the light station. Seen in this photograph is a biologist about to rescue an elephant seal that was half buried in sand while he slept. (Courtesy PBLS Collection/Hatfield.)

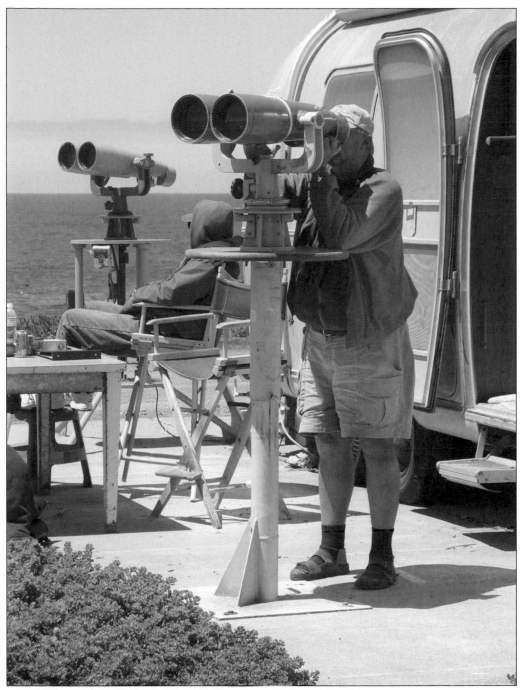

Grey whale research began at Piedras Blancas in 1980 by Michael Pool. After a brief respite, it continues today under the auspices of the National Marine Fisheries Service. Every spring, biologists count the number of gray whale mothers and calves that pass Point Piedras Blancas. Pictured at the large binoculars referred to as "big eyes" is Richard Rowlett. (Courtesy PBLS Collection.)

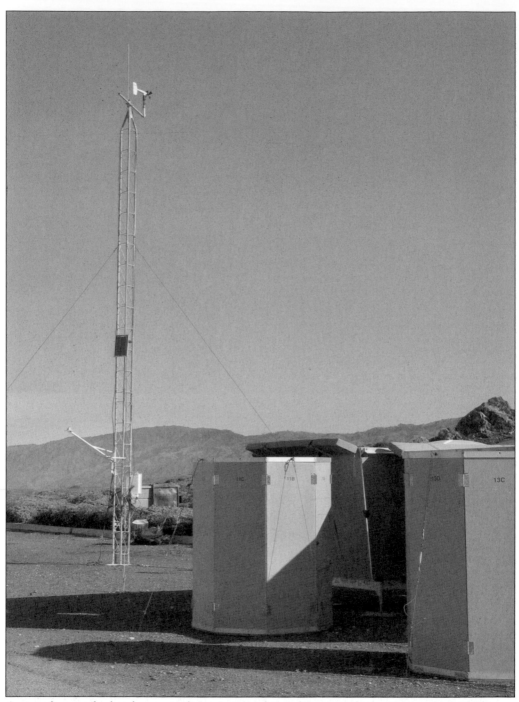

Areas of research that began under coast guard jurisdiction and continue at Piedras Blancas currently include tide pool research by PISCO and atmospheric testing by NOAA. Every winter, NOAA sets up an unmanned station to monitor upper atmospheric conditions. The information is relayed directly to offices in Colorado. (Courtesy PBLS Collection.)

Four

Bureau of Land Management
2001–Present

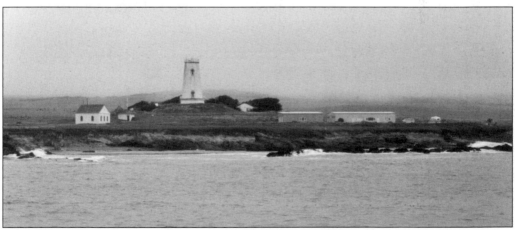

In the fall of 2001, the U.S. Department of the Interior, Bureau of Land Management assumed management of the Piedras Blancas Light Station. The site was in poor condition and dramatically altered from its historic appearance. BLM staff, partners, and volunteers are hard at work transforming the site back to its original glory and will eventually reopen the site full-time to the public. A snapshot of these efforts is contained within this chapter. (Courtesy PBLS Collection.)

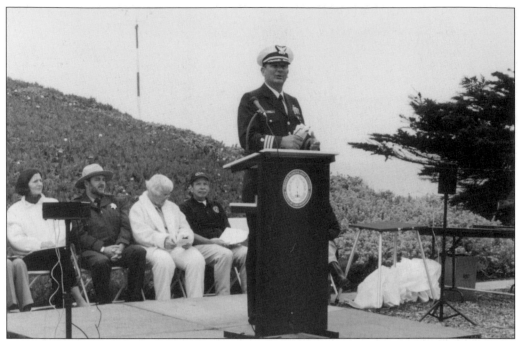

On May 22, 2001, management responsibility was transferred from the U.S. Coast Guard to the Bureau of Land Management in an official change of command ceremony held at the light station. (Courtesy PBLS Collection.)

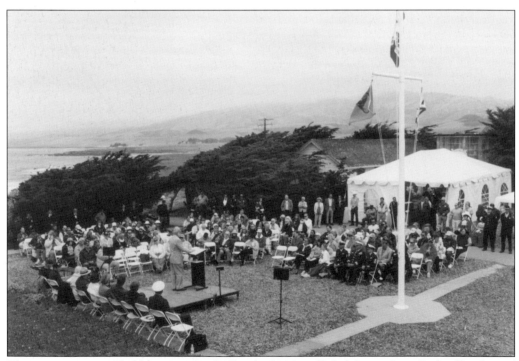

The event was attended by coast guard officials, BLM staff, California State Park officials, and members of the community. (Courtesy PBLS Collection.)

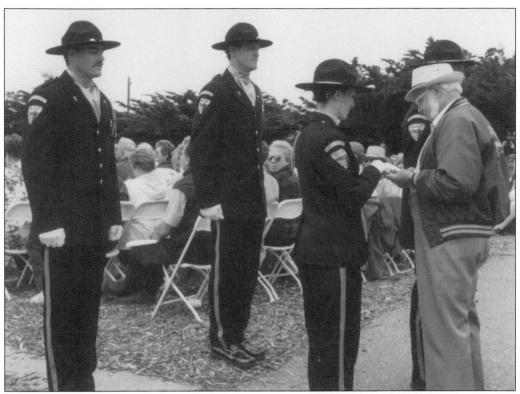

World War II veteran coast guard seaman Jim Lilly was presented with the traditional U.S. Lighthouse Service pennant by the BLM color guard. Lilly raised the pennant during the ceremony. He served at the Piedras Blancas Light Station from 1945 to 1947. (Courtesy PBLS Collection.)

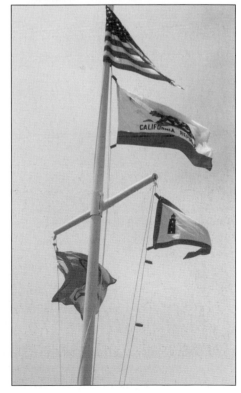

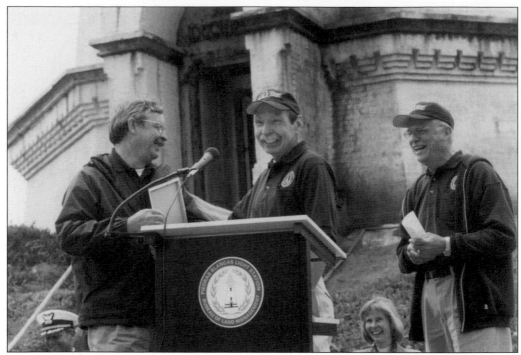

BLM managers John Bogacki, Bakersfield Field Office manager Ron Fellows, and former BLM manager Bob Rheiner enjoy a light moment during the official "change of command" ceremony. Rep. Lois Capps (D) of Santa Barbara, in whose district PBLS is located, is seated behind them. (Courtesy PBLS Collection.)

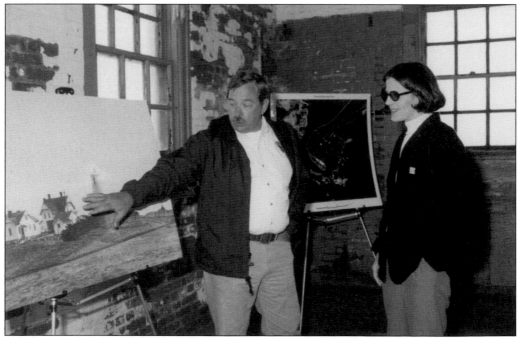

BLM site manager John Bogacki gives Assistant Secretary of the Interior Lyn Scarlett a tour of the facilities, explaining the history of the site and plans for restoration. (Courtesy PBLS Collection.)

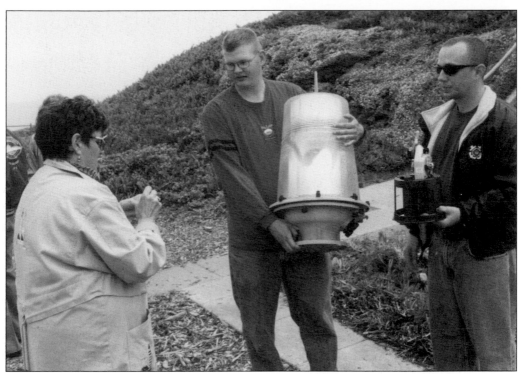

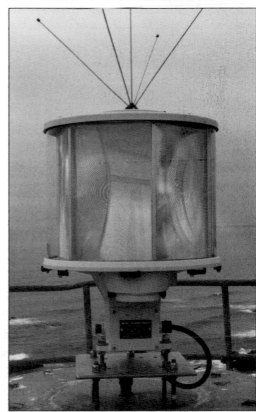

On the day before the ceremony, the dim emergency light was removed and replaced with a new 800,000-candlepower VRB 25 beacon, seen at right. Above, Cambrian reporter Kathe Tanner interviews coast guard seamen who assisted BLM personnel in installing the new light. (Courtesy PBLS Collection.)

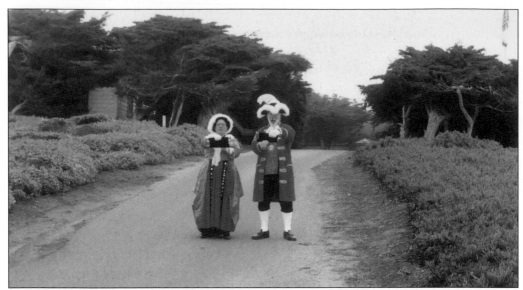

One of the first priorities the BLM identified was to introduce the public to this unique site. The first public tour offered by the BLM was given in June 2004. Cambria town criers Beverly and Jerry Praver heralded the event with a special cry. (Courtesy PBLS Collection.)

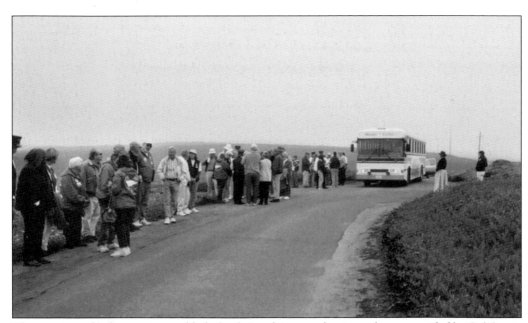

The guests on the first tour assembled after being driven to the site on buses provided by California State Parks at Hearst Castle. Ticket arrangements were made through the National Geographic Theater, also located at Hearst Castle. (Courtesy PBLS Collection.)

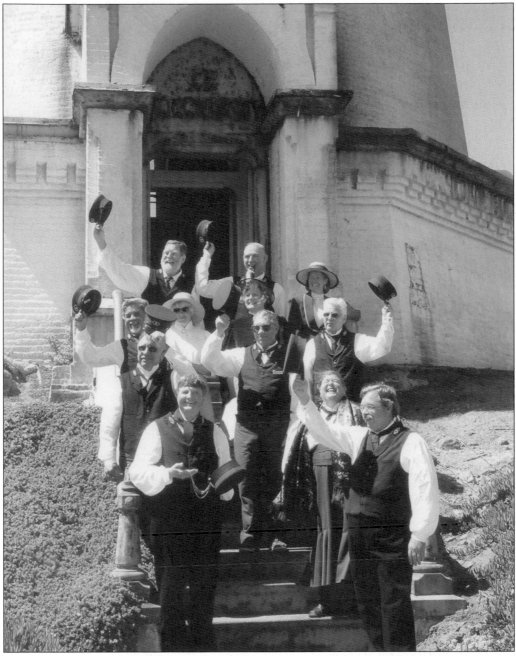

BLM tour guides and interpreters dress in 1890 period dress. (Courtesy PBLS Collection.)

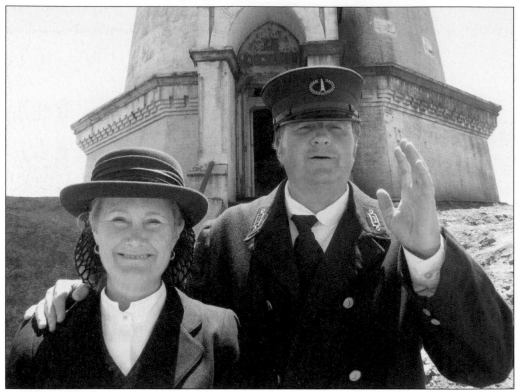

Shawn and Penny Harris were instrumental in setting up the first public tour program. Shawn developed the interpretive walk and coordinated the tours. Penny researched and assembled the period clothing wardrobe and established standards to ensure historical accuracy in guide staff attire and mannerisms. (Courtesy PBLS Collection.)

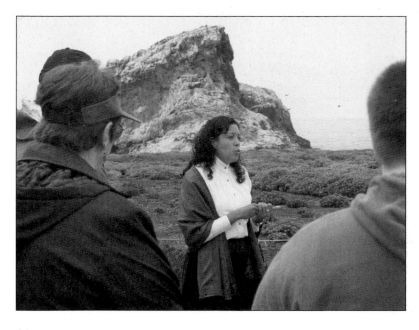

BLM archaeologist Kim Cuevas provides insights into the first people who utilized Point Piedras Blancas. (Courtesy PBLS Collection.)

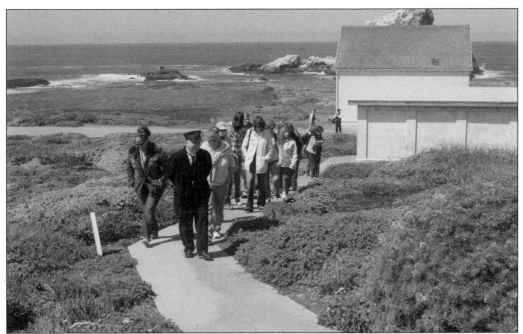

BLM archaeologist Duane Christian leads a public tour past the fuel oil house. Guides present historical information on the light station as well as on cultural, general lighthouse, and maritime history. Programs related to native vegetation and marine mammals are also presented. (Courtesy PBLS Collection.)

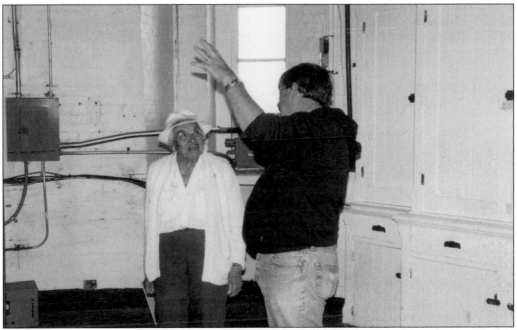

In 2004, John Bogacki escorted Margaret Soto around the site. It was the first time Margaret had visited since 1922, when she was 10 years old. Margaret remembered that the children were admonished to walk carefully up the stairs to the light and to not touch anything, which was hard to do because the light was so shiny and beautiful. (Courtesy PBLS Collection.)

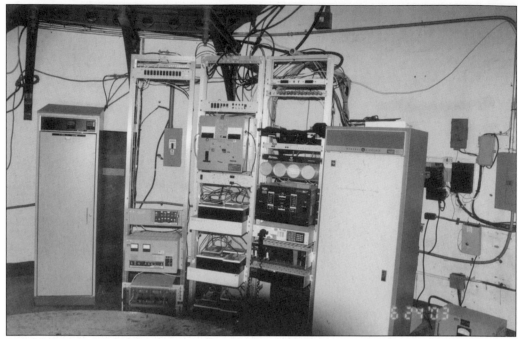

One of the first tasks undertaken on the road to restoration was the removal of communications equipment from the rotunda of the lighthouse (above) to a more appropriate site. In 2005, a new communications center was created, eliminating the need to have equipment located in the lighthouse. This new location (below) houses public safety and weather monitoring equipment. (Courtesy PBLS Collection.)

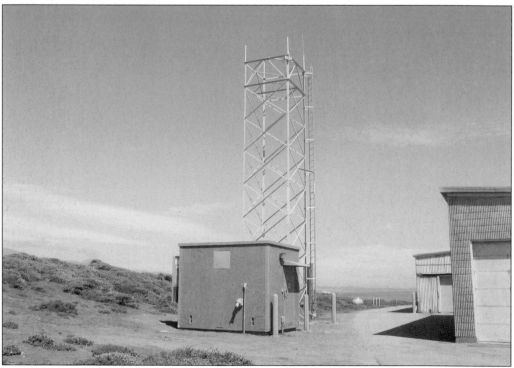

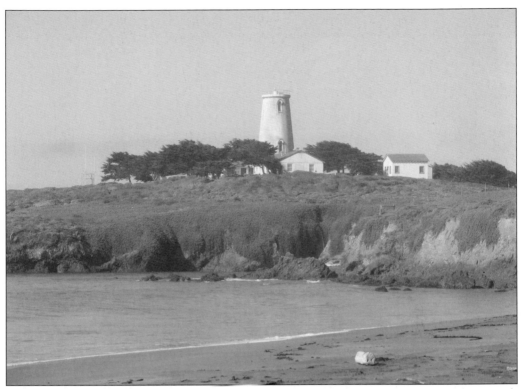

The view from the south in 2005 shows the lighthouse without the antennae. In the photograph below, the tank house, where the water storage tank is located, can be seen in the foreground. The arm at the top of the lighthouse serves as a perch for the peregrine falcons. (Courtesy PBLS Collection.)

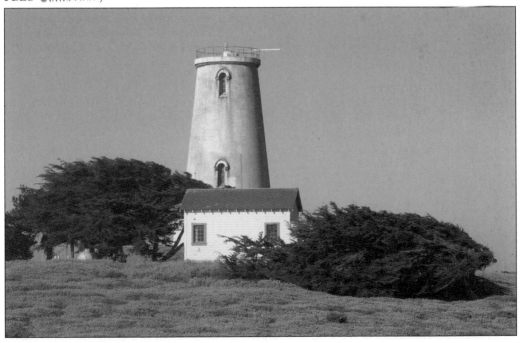

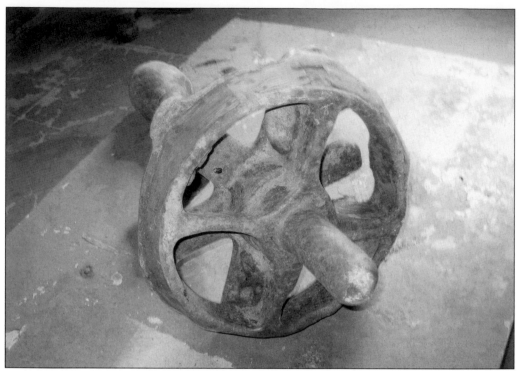

As the face of the site changed over the years, equipment and structures became obsolete and were often removed. Some of the equipment was tossed over the bluff into the ocean. A remnant of one of the old engines, used to generate compressed air for the sound signal, was found on the beach in June 2007 and returned to the fog signal building. The artifact is the crankshaft and portion of the flywheel from the Hornsby-Akroyd oil engine. (Courtesy PBLS Collection.)

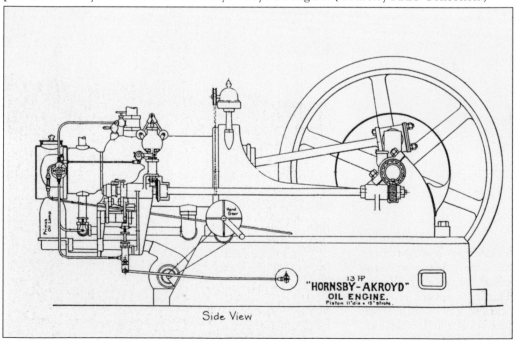

"HORNSBY-AKROYD" OIL ENGINE.

Side View

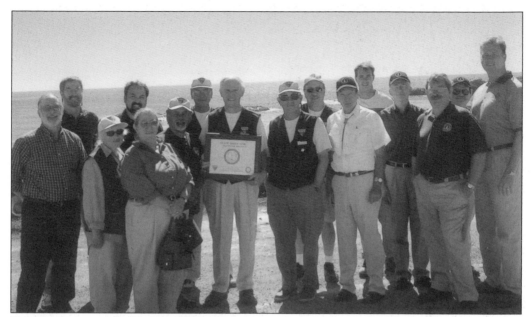

Volunteers play a pivotal role in BLM's efforts to restore the site to its period of historic significance. Important contributions have been made by the site's volunteer corps on many fronts, including historical research, archival work, native plant restoration, tour management, and maintenance. In 2004, volunteers at Piedras Blancas received an award from Mike Pool, BLM California state director (far right). (Courtesy PBLS Collection.)

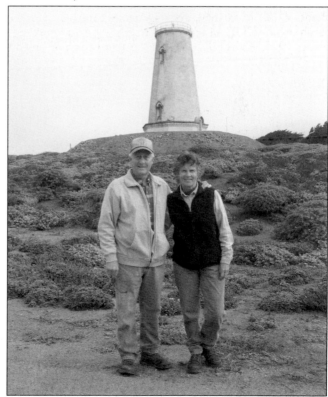

Volunteers Bob and Marsha Goss typify the hardworking, dedicated spirit of the Piedras Blancas volunteers. They have contributed to many areas of endeavor at the light station. (Courtesy PBLS Collection.)

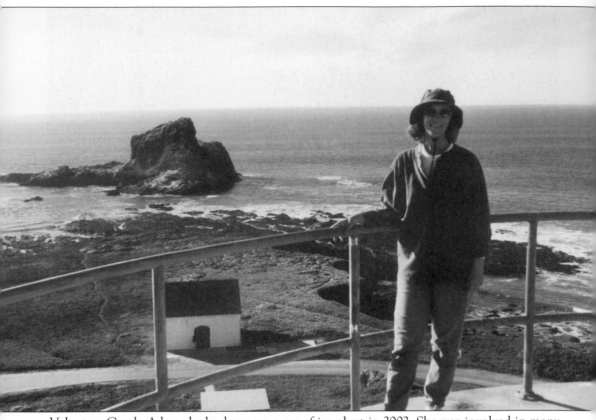

Volunteer Carole Adams looks down on a sea of ice plant in 2002. She was involved in many volunteer activities at Piedras Blancas. In 2004, she earned the prestigious Making a Difference award from BLM, which she received in Washington, D.C., for her work in native plant restoration and other projects. (Courtesy PBLS Collection.)

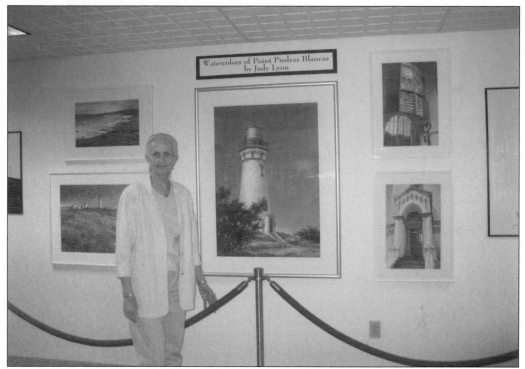

Judy Lyon's beautiful watercolors of the Piedras Blancas Light Station have been featured in two displays at the Hearst Castle National Geographic Theater. She has generously granted reproduction rights of these images to the Piedras Blancas Light Station Association. (Courtesy PBLS Collection.)

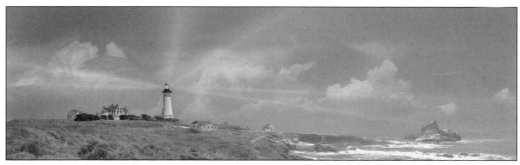

Volunteer Mark Arnold has created several computer enhanced photographs that focus on the Piedras Blancas first-order Fresnel light casting beams into the sky. Seen here is the double flash light characteristic in a physical setting appropriate to the 1930s–1940s. (Courtesy Mark Arnold.)

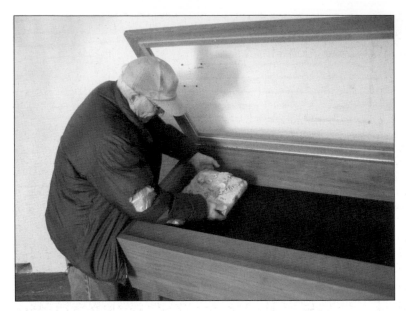

Will Dallons is a master woodworker. As volunteers, he and his wife, Suzanne, have created many items for the Piedras Blancas Light Station. At left, he is seen placing the first shipwreck artifact, a barnacle-encrusted tile from the *Harlech Castle*, in one of the lovely display cases he built. (Courtesy PBLS Collection.)

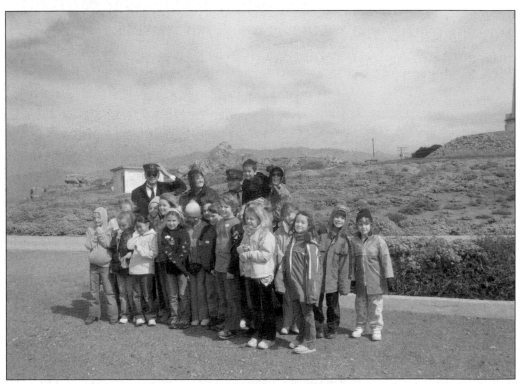

A second- and third-grade class from Grover Heights Elementary School in Grover Beach began raising money to aid in the restoration of the Piedras Blancas Light Station in 2005. The project was dubbed "Pennies for Piedras" by student Conner Sandman, who came up with the idea when he realized the top was missing from the lighthouse he chose to study. Led by super-teacher Libby Anderson, who is also a lighthouse buff, the students raised over $3,000 in two years. (Courtesy PBLS Collection.)

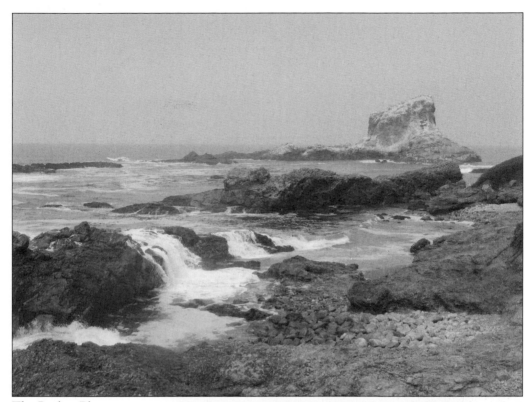

The Piedras Blancas
Light Station serves as a
gateway to the California
Coastal National
Monument, which is also
managed by the BLM.
The monument was
created in 2000 and is
comprised of rocks and
islands off the California
coastline reaching from
the Mexican border to
Oregon. In 2006, the four
large rocks off Piedras
Blancas were donated to
the BLM by the Hearst
Corporation for inclusion
in the California Coastal
National Monument.
At right, Steven Hearst
is presented with a
photograph of the Outer
Islet by BLM state director
Mike Pool. (Courtesy
PBLS Collection.)

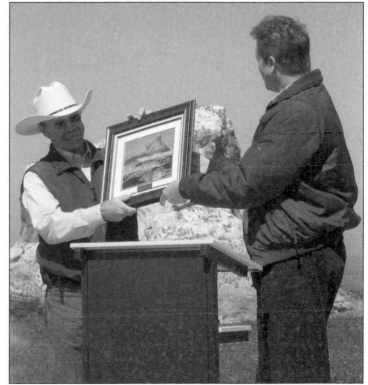

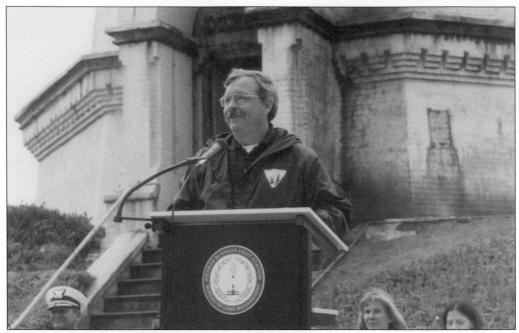

In January 2007, John Bogacki retired as manager of the Piedras Blancas Light Station. He helped to create the foundation of community and volunteer participation at the Piedras Blancas Light Station and wrote the proposed management plan. (Courtesy PBLS Collection.)

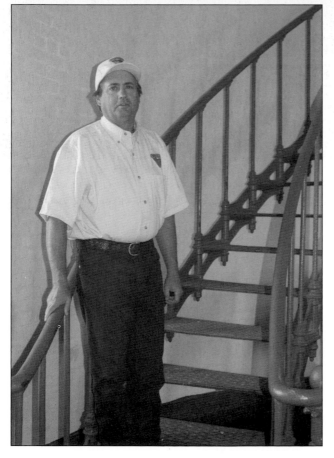

Jim Boucher took over the role of manager in January 2007. Boucher is actively moving the site forward toward restoration and greater public access. He is pictured standing on the bottom rungs of the original stairs within the lighthouse. (Courtesy PBLS Collection.)

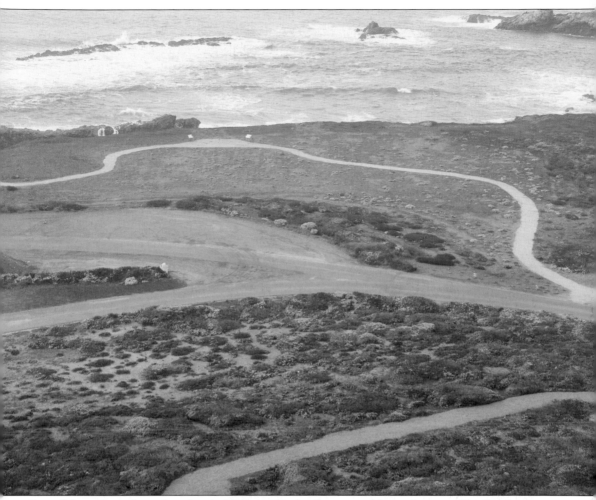

One of the major tasks undertaken in 2007 was the development of the trail system. The California Civilian Conservation Corps provided much needed labor and assistance in the development of this trail. Also assisting in the trailblazing efforts were members of the Student Conservation Association. (Courtesy PBLS Collection.)

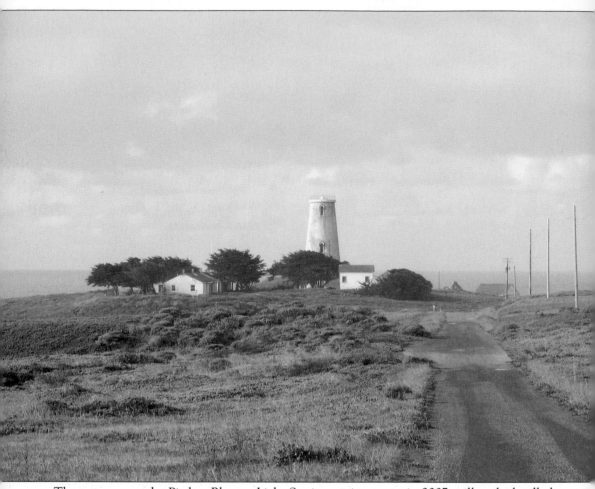

The entrance to the Piedras Blancas Light Station, as it appears in 2007, will undoubtedly be changing as restoration efforts continue to take place. (Courtesy PBLS Collection.)

Five

PLANS FOR THE FUTURE

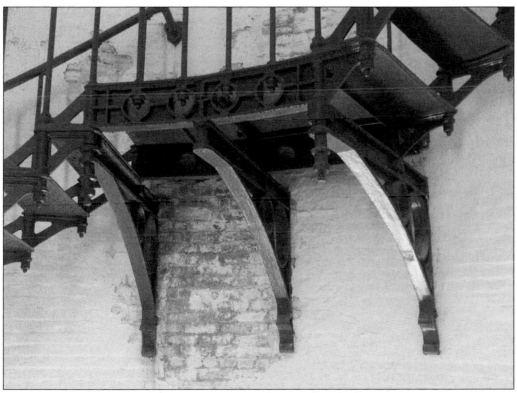

Classic but nonetheless standard lighthouse ironwork as seen in many brick masonry towers stands out in the Piedras Blancas Lighthouse. Earthquakes, poor maintenance, and harsh weather have seriously impacted the integrity of these features, which will be subject to a complete engineering analysis, repair, and restoration. (Courtesy PBLS Collection.)

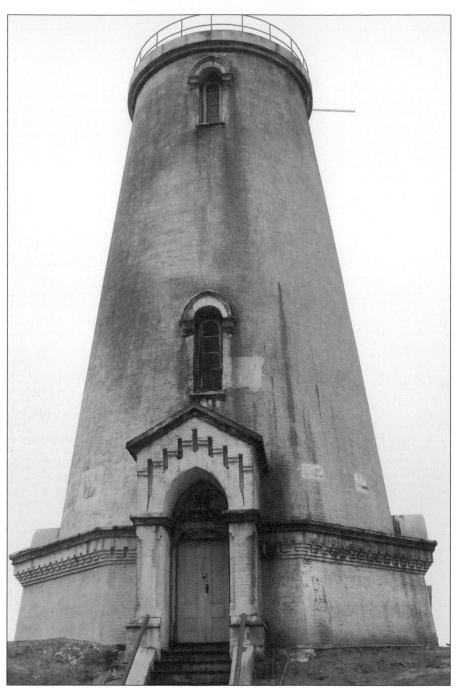

Gothic, neoclassical, and Romanesque architectural features make this once-proud lighthouse an outstanding example of lighthouse art. Missing elements include the fourth landing, watch room, and lantern room, all of which will be replaced during restoration. The dark coloration shown in this photograph is the result of iron stains, mold, and wind-driven silt. The restored lighthouse will feature white masonry accented with black, cast-iron ornamentation. Even without the missing features, the lighthouse was determined to be eligible and placed on the National Register of Historic Places. (Courtesy PBLS Collection.)

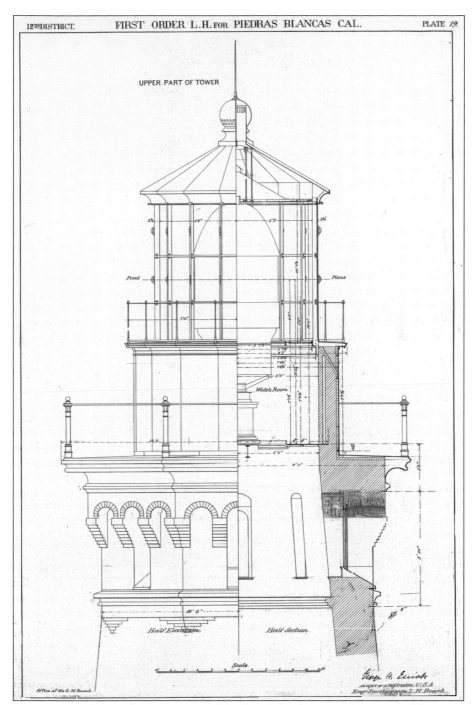

UPPER PART OF TOWER

Focal   *Plane*

Watch Room

Half Elevation.   *Half Section.*

Scale

Office of the L.H. Board.

Engr Secretary to the L. H Board.

This is an original drawing/cutaway view of the fourth landing, watch room, and lantern room. Note the ornamental styling in the brickwork. The U.S. Lighthouse Establishment standardized the drawings for many lighthouse components and features. The watch room and lantern room for the Piedras Blancas Lighthouse are identical to many other first-order watch room/lantern rooms such as Point Sur, Point Conception, and Point Reyes Lighthouses. This is the portion of the lighthouse that will be reconstructed as part of restoration. (Courtesy PBLS Collection.)

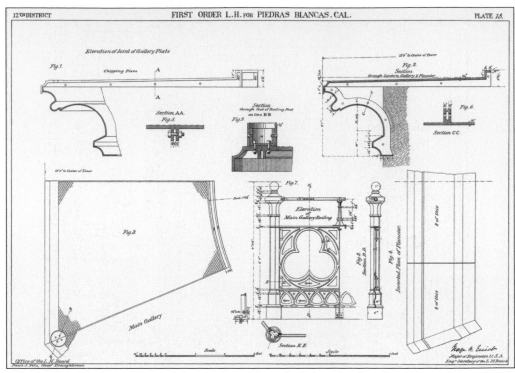

The top plate illustrates some of the cast-iron gallery deck, hand rail, and springer molding details unique to Piedras Blancas. These and other cast-iron components will be faithfully reproduced using modern foundry practices and quality control to ensure accurate and structurally sound component reproduction. The bottom plate shows a comparison of the original configuration (right) and the altered or present configuration after the topmost portions were damaged and removed after an earthquake in late 1948. The Bureau of Land Management has gone to considerable effort to ensure that the quality of the restoration effort is accurate while meeting modern seismic and structural standards. (Courtesy PBLS Collection.)

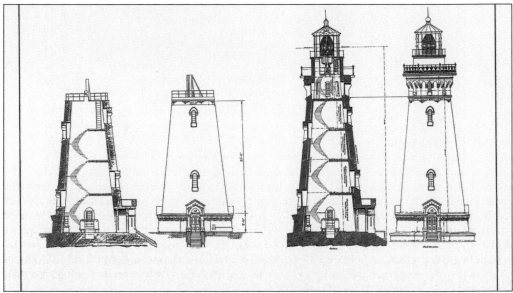

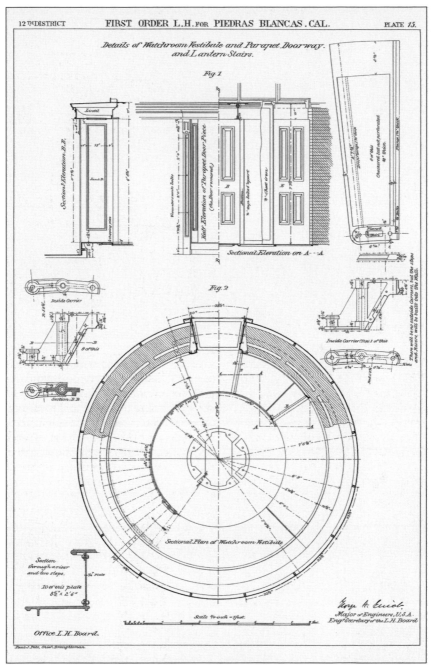

Details of Watchroom Vestibule and Parapet Doorway.
and Lantern Stairs.

Fig. 1

Fig. 2

Sectional Plan of Watchroom Vestibule

Office L.H. Board.

Major of Engineers, U.S.A.
Eng'r Secretary of the L.H. Board

This plate illustrates a portion of the watch room vestibule, parapet doorway, and lantern stair arrangements. Early foundry practices sometimes produced components of variable quality, which could over the years create problems with structural integrity because of exposure to extreme weather conditions, earthquakes, and so forth. Modern engineering and foundry practices as applied to lighthouse restoration produce components that are both historically accurate and provide a high degree of structural integrity. Designers will utilize these drawings to create engineering and foundry drawings used to fabricate the new elements and to replace broken or highly eroded components. (Courtesy PBLS Collection.)

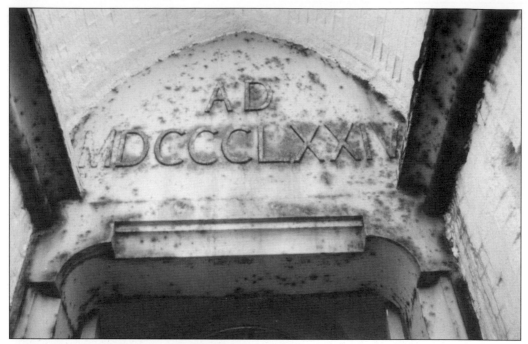

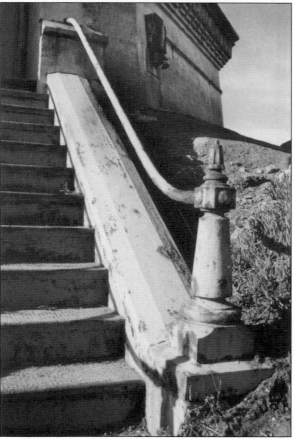

While much of the existing cast-iron ornamentation is badly damaged or corroded, some of the features exhibit outstanding detail, which will be retained and carefully restored. The photograph above shows the cast-iron inscription plate, which displays the date 1874 (in Roman numerals), the year the lighthouse construction began. Also note the finely cast details designed into the door jams and lintel. The photograph at left shows a portion of the cast-iron stairs leading into the lighthouse. The handrail is a mid-1970s repair that will be removed and replaced with an accurate reproduction of the original handrail. (Courtesy PBLS Collection.)

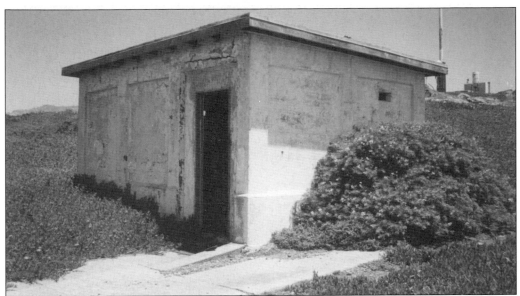

The site's other two National Register properties are shown here. The top photograph is the fuel oil house, constructed in 1907. It was deemed necessary when the lighthouse fuel source was changed from lard oil to mineral oil (kerosene), which is more volatile, requiring segregated storage. This building was one of the first reinforced concrete buildings constructed by the federal government on the West Coast. Concrete was just coming into accepted use, and these small buildings were ideal candidates for its use. Far more architecturally significant, however, is the fog signal building (bottom) constructed in 1906. It is a brick masonry structure with an exposed wooden truss-supported roof. It housed the station's fog signal apparatus, which remained in use until 1974. It, too, is scheduled to be completely restored for use as the site's education and interpretive center. (Courtesy PBLS Collection.)

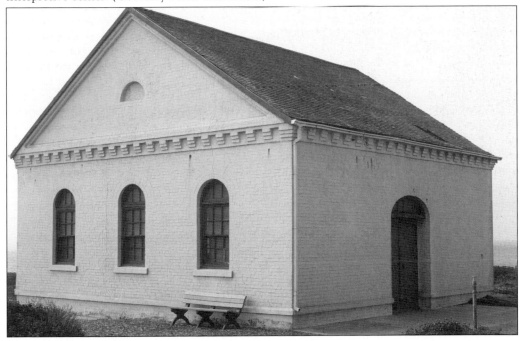

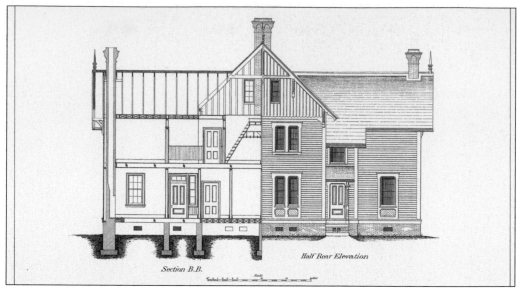

Section B.B.   *Half Rear Elevation*

These plates illustrate the keeper's triplex or multifamily dwelling. It was constructed in 1876 as a duplex, but it was used to house three families. This dwelling was built at three different light stations. The other two locations were on the East Coast. Where possible and/or appropriate, the U.S. Lighthouse Establishment reused existing plans to keep design costs to a minimum. This dwelling served the site until 1960, when both it and the head keeper's dwelling were removed to make way for more contemporary housing. The triplex was demolished using two D-4 bulldozers. It took two days to demolish this dwelling. The head keeper's dwelling was moved into the nearby village of Cambria, where it now serves as a vacation rental. Both of these dwellings would be reconstructed under the BLM's recently approved management plan. (Courtesy PBLS Collection.)

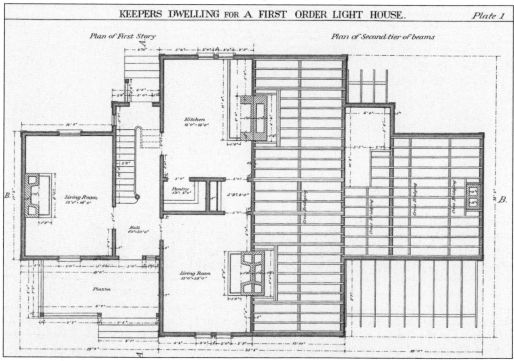

KEEPERS DWELLING FOR A FIRST ORDER LIGHT HOUSE.   *Plate 1*

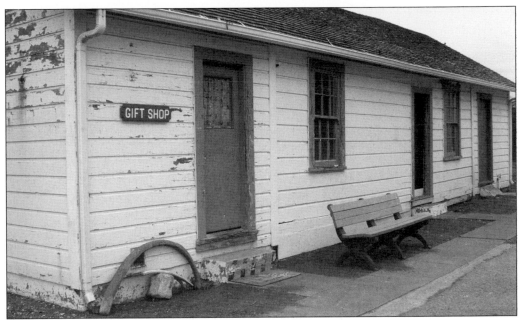

The fuel and storage building sat behind or west of the keeper's triplex. When it was originally constructed in 1876, it was used to store personal items and the supply of coal used to heat the house and for use in the cook stoves. In 1935, it was lengthened to convert it to a shop and office for the site. Keepers utilized whatever space was available for shops, storage, and administrative needs. This structure will be restored and utilized as a gift shop and/or administrative spaces for the site when completed. (Courtesy PBLS Collection.)

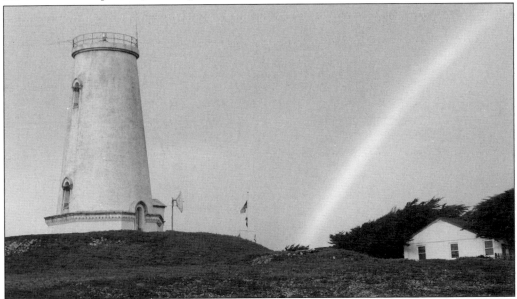

This photograph shows the existing contemporary housing that will eventually be removed to make way for the historic reconstruction of the original dwellings. Much of the nonnative plants shown have been removed to allow natural plant growth to take place. The communications equipment on the lighthouse, including the microwave dish, has been removed to another, less obtrusive location. (Courtesy PBLS Collection.)

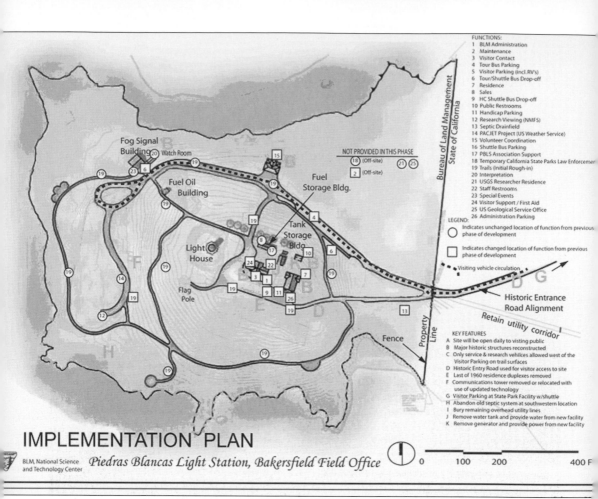

FUNCTIONS:
1 BLM Administration
2 Maintenance
3 Visitor Contact
4 Tour Bus Parking
5 Visitor Parking (incl. RV's)
6 Tour/Shuttle Bus Drop-off
7 Residence
8 Sales
9 HC Shuttle Bus Drop-off
10 Public Restrooms
11 Handicap Parking
12 Research Viewing (NMFS)
13 Septic Drainfield
14 PACJET Project (US Weather Service)
15 Volunteer Coordination
16 Shuttle Bus Parking
17 PBLS Association Support
18 Temporary California State Parks Law Enforcement
19 Trails (Initial Rough-in)
20 Interpretation
21 USGS Researcher Residence
22 Staff Restrooms
23 Special Events
24 Visitor Support / First Aid
25 US Geological Service Office
26 Administration Parking

LEGEND:
○ Indicates unchanged location of function from previous phase of development
□ Indicates changed location of function from previous phase of development
▪ ▪ ▪ Visiting vehicle circulation

KEY FEATURES
A Site will be open daily to visiting public
B Major historic structures reconstructed
C Only service & research vehilces allowed west of the Visitor Parking on trail surfaces
D Historic Entry Road used for visitor access to site
E Last of 1960 residence duplexes removed
F Communications tower removed or relocated with use of updated technology
G Visitor Parking at State Park Facility w/shuttle
H Abandon old septic system at southwestern location
I Bury remaining overhead utility lines
J Remove water tank and provide water from new facility
K Remove generator and provide power from new facility

Bureau of Land Management
State of California

Fog Signal Building
Watch Room
Fuel Oil Building
Fuel Storage Bldg.
Tank Storage Bldg
Light House
Flag Pole
Fence
Property Line
Historic Entrance Road Alignment
Retain utility corridor

NOT PROVIDED IN THIS PHASE
18 (Off-site)
2 (Off-site)

IMPLEMENTATION PLAN

BLM National Science and Technology Center *Piedras Blancas Light Station, Bakersfield Field Office*

0   100   200   400 F

This illustration, taken from the management plan, shows the extent to which the site will be restored and rehabilitated. Some key features include restoration or replacement of structures and features that would have been present during the period of historic significance (1874–1940). Other features will include universal accessibility, unlimited view shed, and state-of-the-art visitor services, education, and transportation improvements. (Courtesy PBLS Collection.)

Six

NATIVE PLANT
RESTORATION

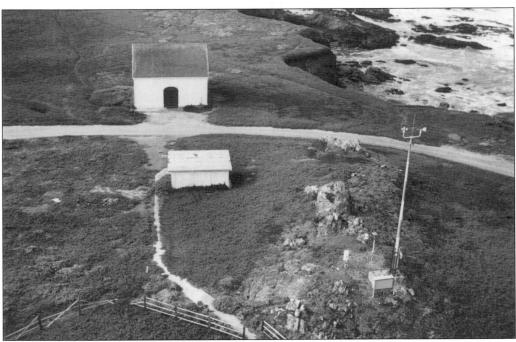

When the BLM assumed management of the Piedras Blancas Light Station, ice plant planted between 1940 and 1970 had completely taken over the native vegetation. Ice plant (*Carpobrutus sp.*), which is native to South Africa, was extremely invasive and was growing up the sides of the buildings, covering walkways, and choking out native vegetation. In addition to ice plant, there were approximately 40 other species of nonnative plants on the site. In evaluating plans for restoration, the decision was made to return native vegetation to the site, as it would have appeared before and during the site's period of historic significance. This daunting task was given to the site's volunteer cadre, who tackled the challenge with unprecedented enthusiasm. (Courtesy PBLS Collection.)

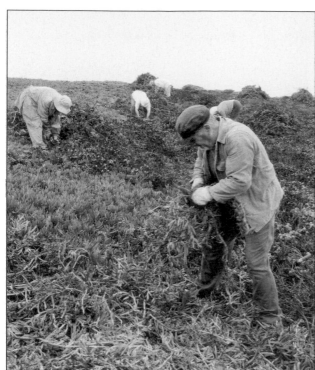

Guided by BLM botanist Russ Lewis and other native plant experts, volunteers began removing ice plant and other nonnative plants by hand-pulling unwanted vegetation from areas of existing native plants. Care was taken to not disturb the soil because the entire 19 acres is an archaeological site. The volunteers refer to it as "a big weeding job." In the foreground are volunteers Toni and Abel Martinez. (Courtesy PBLS Collection.)

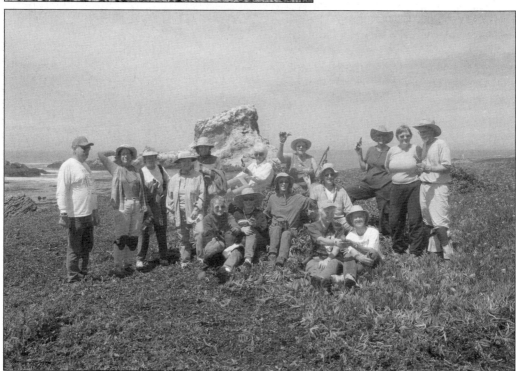

Community groups also came out to help. As the saying goes, many hands make light work. Well, maybe the work isn't light, but many hands make it fun and get the job done faster. (Courtesy PBLS Collection.)

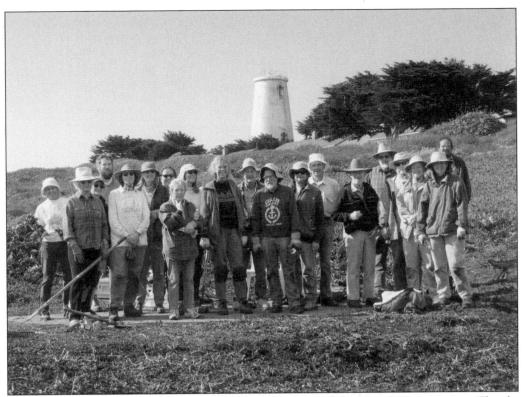

Above, Piedras Blancas volunteers are joined by members of the Native Plant Society. Thanks are due to everyone who came out to help over the years. Included in this photograph are several people who acted as advisors during the initial stages of the effort: Jack Beigle (volunteer extraordinaire, seventh from right), and Cal Poly botanists Malcolm McLeod (sixth from right) and Dirk Walters (fifth from right). (Courtesy PBLS Collection.)

One of the first native plants to appear in cleared areas is the rare compact cobwebby thistle (*Cirsium occidentale* var. *compactum*). A BLM botanist only found one individual plant on the site in 2001, but within a few years, there were hundreds germinating. In the spring of 2007, a grand total of 1,000 plants were counted, amounting to a 1,000-percent increase. (Courtesy PBLS Collection.)

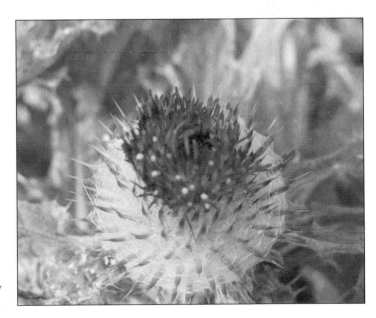

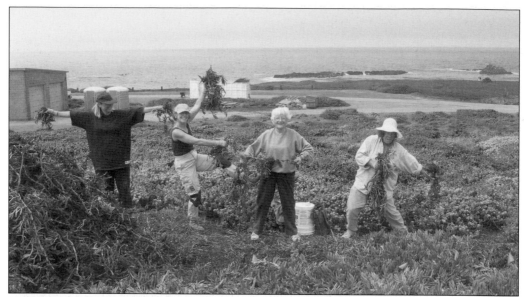

Piedras Blancas cheerleaders Leslie McGarry, Beverly Hardwick, and Dorothy and Elizabeth Bettenhausen generated enthusiasm and positive energy, necessary ingredients to getting the job done. They are spelling out the word "team." (Courtesy PBLS Collection.)

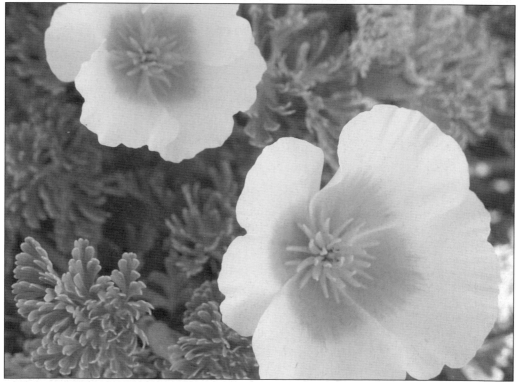

Also cheering on the work were profusions of seaside poppies (*Eschscholzia californica* var. *maritima*). This lovely variation of the more commonly known California state flower is brilliant orange in the center of the blossom and bright yellow on the outside. About 70 native plant species have been identified at Point Piedras Blancas. (Courtesy PBLS Collection.)

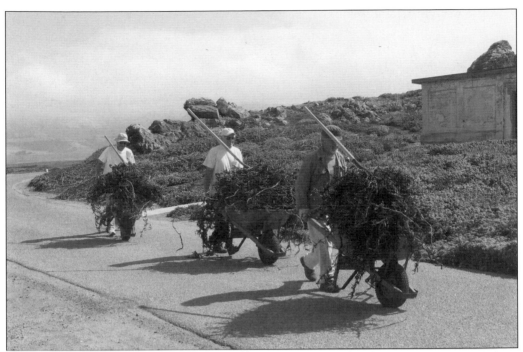

Wheelbarrows, trucks, and other means of transportation were used to remove dried ice plant. As soon as the ice plant was removed, native plants began emerging from long-dormant seedbeds in the soil. (Courtesy PBLS Collection.)

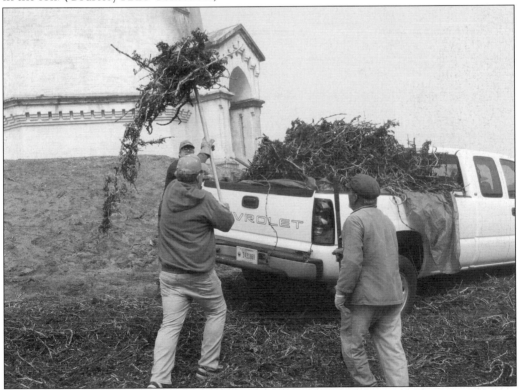

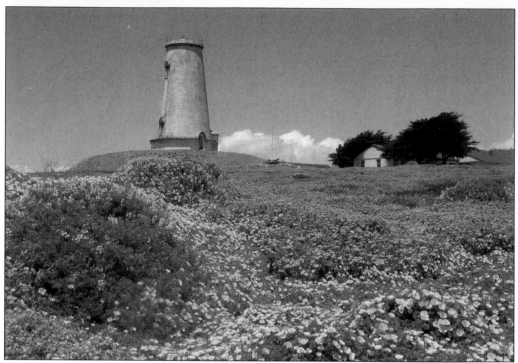

Native plants filled in quickly. During spring, the smell of lupine fills the air. (Courtesy PBLS Collection.)

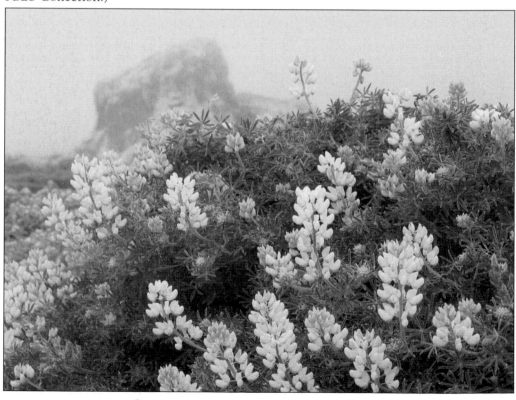

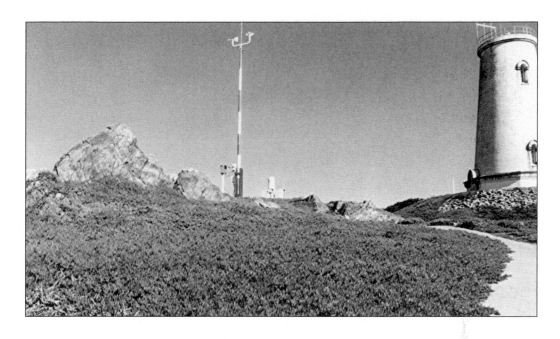

The photograph above was taken in 2002. Ice plant dominates the landscape. The photograph below was taken in 2005. Native plants now thrive in areas formerly covered in ice plant. (Courtesy PBLS Collection.)

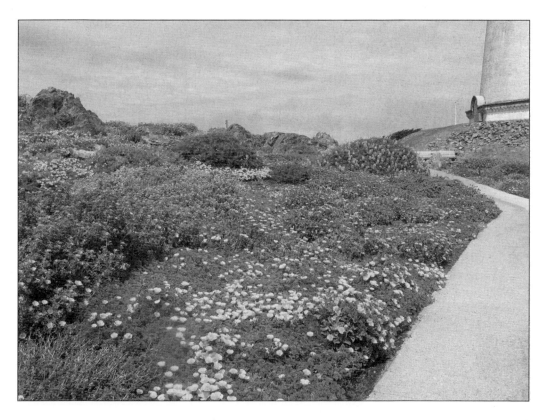

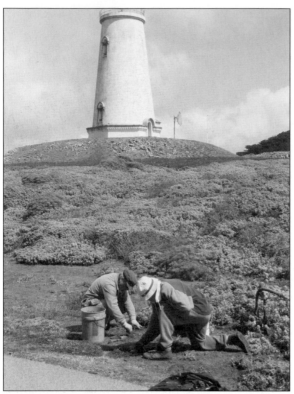

Pulling ice plant is only the first part of the process. The other nonnative plant species that germinate after the ice plant is pulled must also be removed for progress to occur. Abel Martinez and Bruce Marchese cull out unwanted species. (Courtesy PBLS Collection.)

The Piedras Blancas detail weeders are worth their weight in gold. Below, Toni Moore painstakingly removes nonnative plants before they take over an especially beautiful area nicknamed the Rocky Knoll. (Courtesy PBLS Collection.)

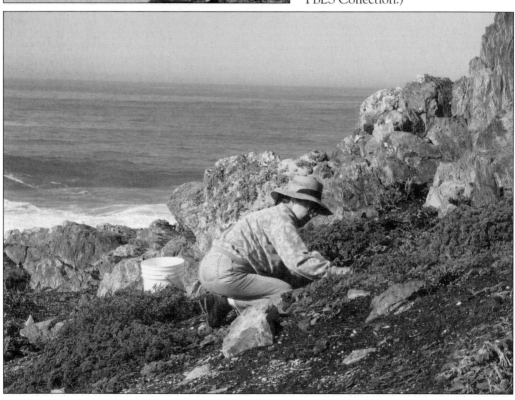

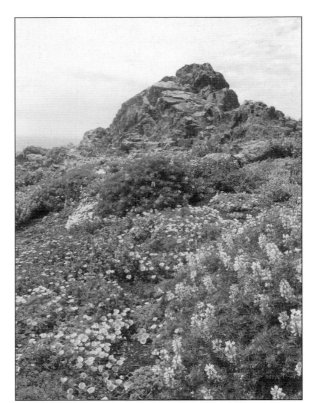

Where there was once ice plant, there is now native plant beauty. At right, poppies, tree lupine, and seaside daisies create a blaze of color on the Rocky Knoll. Below, poppies and daisies grace the edging in front of the office. (Courtesy PBLS Collection.)

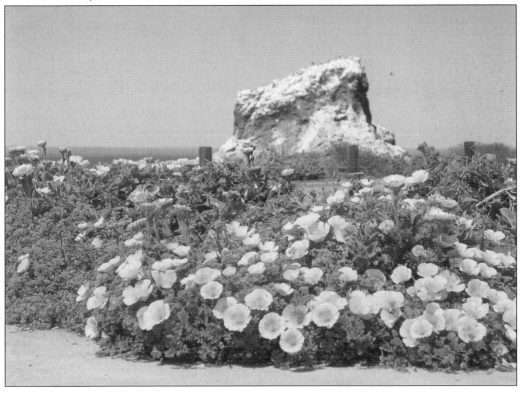

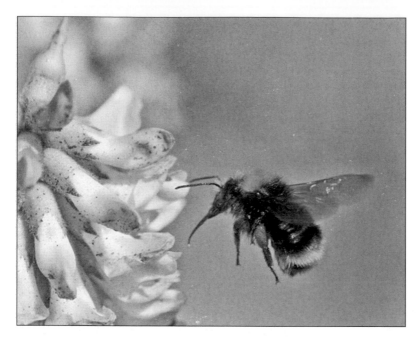

In the native plant areas, there has been an increase in the numbers of birds, small fur-bearing mammals, butterflies, moths, and other insects. (Courtesy Michael L. Baird.)

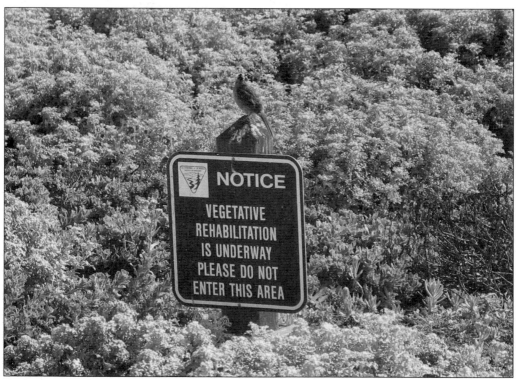

A white-crowned sparrow atop the vegetative rehabilitation sign seems to be expressing his appreciation for the return of native plants to Point Piedras Blancas. (Courtesy PBLS Collection.)

Seven

WILDLIFE

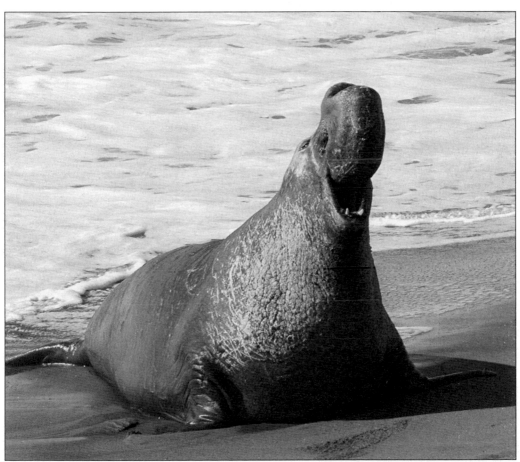

The Piedras Blancas area is a wonderful place to view wildlife. Management efforts at Piedras Blancas are also focused on protecting habitat and encouraging the return of marine mammals and other animals to the site they once inhabited. Above is a big mature male elephant seal trumpeting his arrival after months at sea. (Courtesy Phil Adams.)

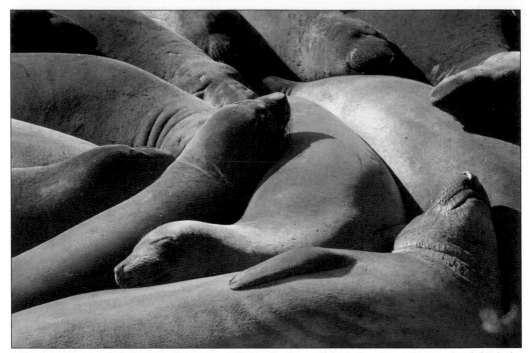

Beginning in the fall of 1990, elephant seals began using the small cove to the south of the light station to come ashore and rest. They continued to return, and in 1992, the first pup was born at Piedras Blancas. In 2007, the number of births was about 4,100, swelling the estimated total rookery population to around 16,000. Piedras Blancas is now the largest mainland elephant seal rookery. (Courtesy Carole Adams.)

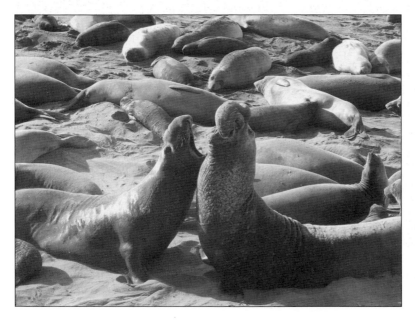

Winter is a busy time at the elephant seal rookery. Males fight for access to females, pups are born and weaned, and mating occurs in preparation for next year's birthing season. (Courtesy Carole Adams.)

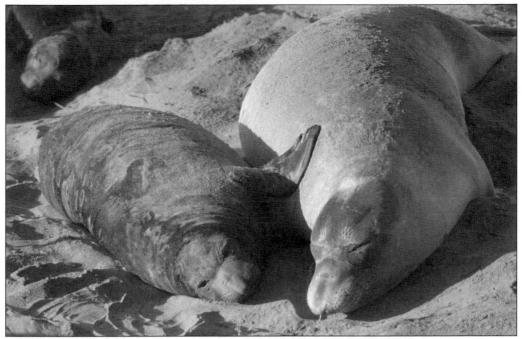

Pups are born weighing 60–80 pounds. They quadruple their weight in less than a month. Just before leaving, the females mate. Pups are left alone to learn how to swim and dive on their own before taking off on their first foraging trip at sea. (Courtesy Phil Adams.)

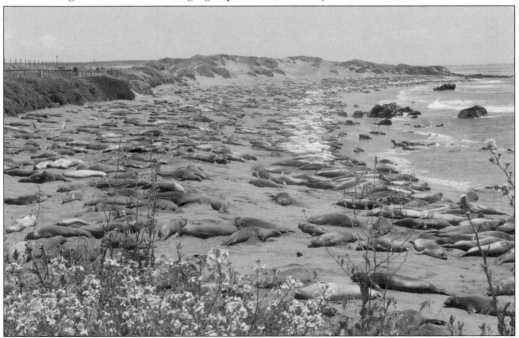

During the spring, large numbers of elephant seals come ashore to molt. This photograph was taken at the official Piedras Blancas elephant seal viewing area, about a mile south of the light station. There docents with Friends of the Elephant Seal are eager to answer questions and enhance the viewing experience. Contact them at www.elephantseal.org. (Courtesy Carole Adams.)

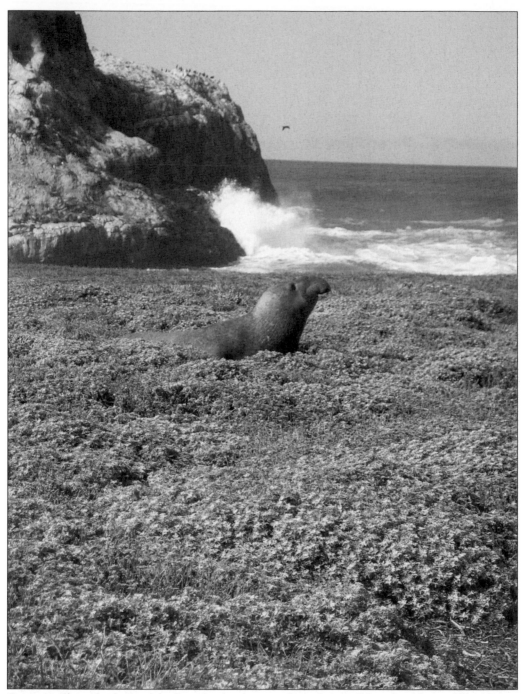

Occasionally male elephant seals make their way up from the south beach and onto light station property. The fellow shown in these photographs was nicknamed "Wrong-way Corrigan." (Courtesy PBLS Collection/Adams.)

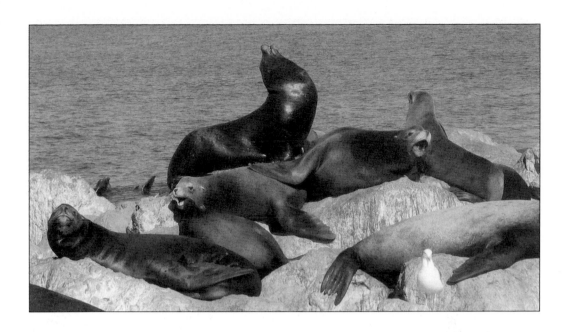

Noisy California sea lions are usually present on the large rocks off Piedras Blancas, especially the Outer Islet. They are often seen leaping out of the water in an activity called "porpoising." On occasion, they may be seen resting in the water with one side flipper and the rear flippers extended into the air. Before there was a sound signal at Piedras Blancas, the sea lions would have alerted ships that they were passing close to rocks. (Courtesy Carole Adams.)

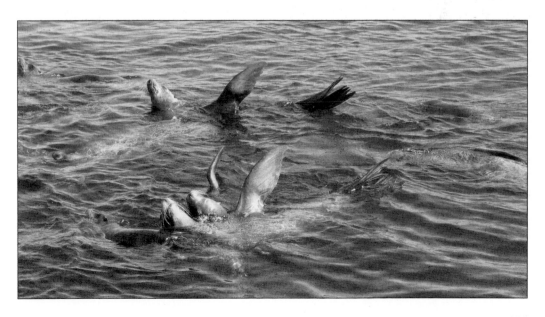

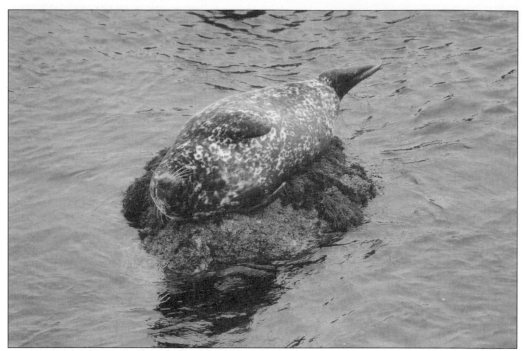

Small sausage-shaped harbor seals may be seen hauling out on low-lying rocks off Point Piedras Blancas at low tide. Harbor seals have small front flippers, no external ear flaps, and are relatively quiet compared to sea lions. (Courtesy Phil Adams.)

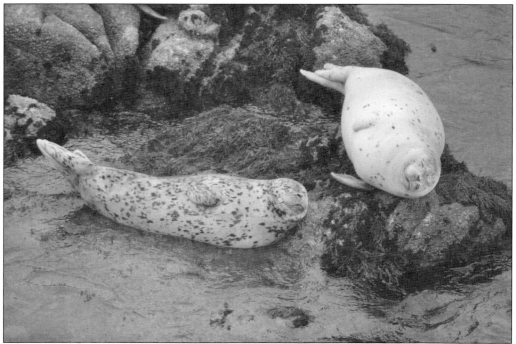

Harbor seals can be light with dark blotches or dark with light blotches. They have short front flippers and no external ear flaps. They are usually shy of people when hauled out on land. Their privacy is protected at Piedras Blancas. (Courtesy Carole Adams.)

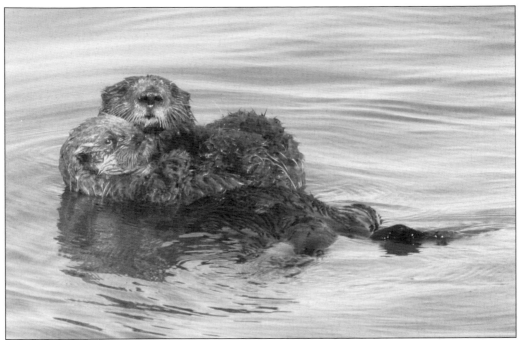

California sea otters may frequently be seen resting in kelp, diving for food, or grooming themselves. Pups ride on their mother's chest and make a high-pitched "ee-ee-ee" sound when trying to get their mother's attention. Sea otters were hunted to the point of extinction by the end of the 1880s for their luxurious fur coats. (Courtesy Michael L. Baird.)

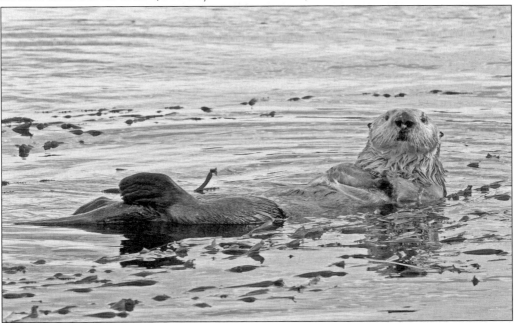

Sea otters have front appendages that are similar to a cat's, while their back appendages are webbed and flipper-like to aid in swimming. They wrap themselves in kelp while sleeping. Sea otters are year-round residents off Piedras Blancas. At times, they haul out on rocks to rest. (Courtesy Michael L. Baird.)

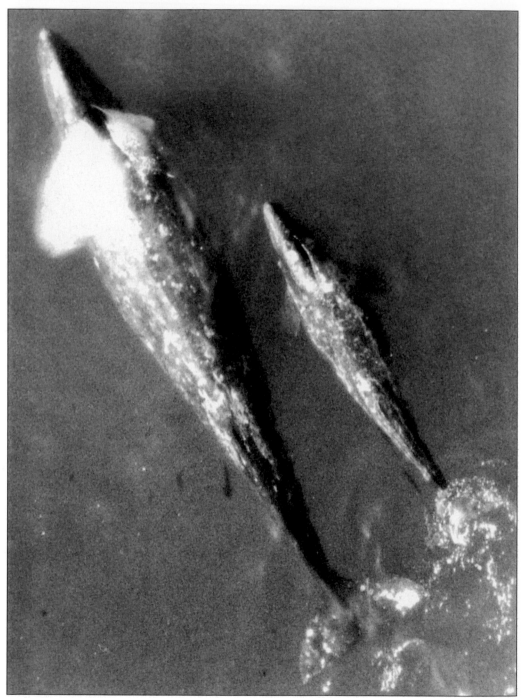

Gray whales migrate past Piedras Blancas from the end of November to the end of May. They travel south in the winter to give birth in the waters off Baja California. In the spring, they head north to feed in the chilly Arctic seas. The mothers and calves travel very close to land as they pass Piedras Blancas in April and May. (Courtesy NMFS.)

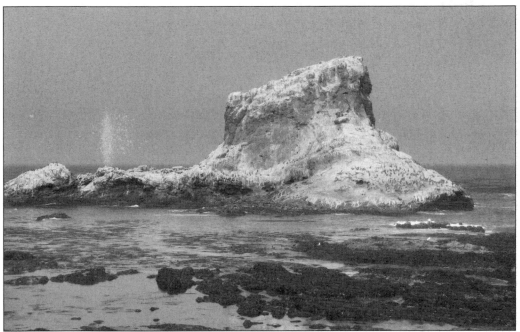

The Outer Islet is used by many marine mammals and birds. Sometimes the rock is almost covered by California sea lions. Four species of birds nest on the Outer Islet: the peregrine falcon, Brandt's cormorant, western gull (below), and black oystercatcher. The white coloration on this rock gave it the name Piedra Blanca, which means "white rock" in Spanish. Piedra Blanca lent its name to the rancho that included this point. Together with the other large white rocks in the vicinity, the area became known as Piedras Blancas, or "white rocks." The white color is the result of accumulations of bird guano, a fact made clear on days that aren't windy. Today this rock is officially called the Outer Islet, although it has also been known by several nicknames, including Lion Rock, Haystack, and Seal Rock. (Above, courtesy PBLS Collection/Adams; below, courtesy Phil Adams.)

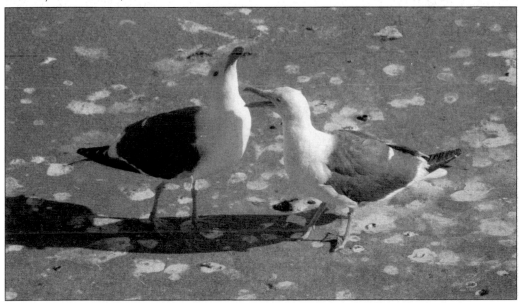

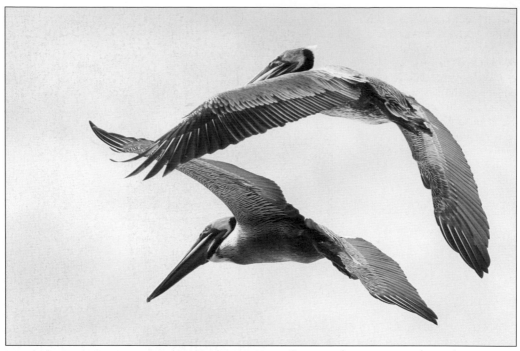

Brown pelicans rest on the rocks off Piedras Blancas. Large groups of these prehistoric-looking birds may be seen resting or flying, especially during the summer months. (Courtesy Michael L. Baird.)

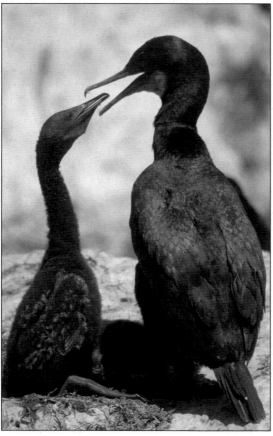

Cormorants, including the Brandt's cormorant, are frequently seen at Piedras Blancas. At left, an adult Brandt's cormorant is feeding a chick. (Courtesy Phil Adams.)

Peregrine falcons nest on the Outer Islet, the large rock west of the point. They can be observed resting on top of the tower or sometimes on one of the window ledges of the lighthouse. (Courtesy Suzanne Dallons.)

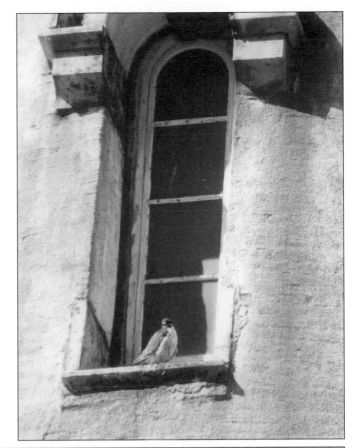

Peregrine flacons are fast, efficient predators, flying at speeds up to 200 miles per hour. They find a lot of prey in the Piedras Blancas area. (Courtesy Michael L. Baird.)

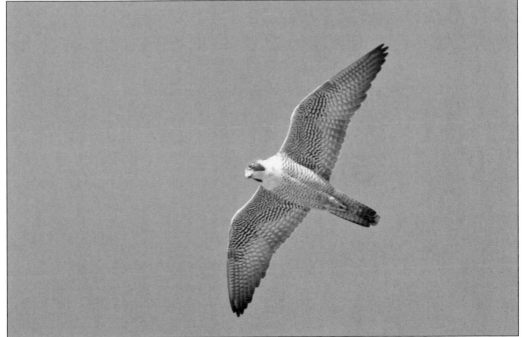

ACROSS AMERICA, PEOPLE ARE DISCOVERING SOMETHING WONDERFUL. *THEIR HERITAGE.*

Arcadia Publishing is the leading local history publisher in the United States. With more than 4,000 titles in print and hundreds of new titles released every year, Arcadia has extensive specialized experience chronicling the history of communities and celebrating America's hidden stories, bringing to life the people, places, and events from the past. To discover the history of other communities across the nation, please visit:

www.arcadiapublishing.com

Customized search tools allow you to find regional history books about the town where you grew up, the cities where your friends and family live, the town where your parents met, or even that retirement spot you've been dreaming about.

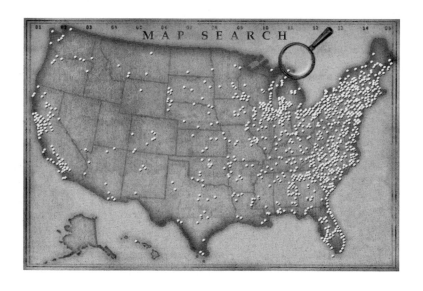